On Becoming
an Innovative
University Teacher

SRHE and Open University Press Imprint
General Editor: Heather Eggins

Current titles include:

On Becoming an Innovative University Teacher

Reflection in Action

John Cowan

The Society for Research into Higher Education
& Open University Press

Published by SRHE and
Open University Press
Celtic Court
22 Ballmoor
Buckingham
MK18 1XW

email: enquiries@openup.co.uk
world wide web: www.openup.co.uk

and
325 Chestnut Street
Philadelphia, PA 19106, USA

First Published 1998
Reprinted 1999, 2000

A catalogue record of this book is available from the British Library

ISBN   0 335 19993 3 (pb)   0 335 19994 1 (hb)

Library of Congress Cataloging-in-Publication Data

Cowan, John, 1932–
    On becoming an innovative university teacher / John Cowan.
      p.   cm.
    Includes bibliographical references and index.
    ISBN   0-335-19994-1 (hardcover). — 0-335-1-9993-3 (pbk.)
    1. College teaching. 2. Reflection (Philosophy)–Study and teaching (Higher) 3. College teachers–Training of. 4. Experiential learning. 5. Educational innovations. I. Title.
LB2331.C68   1998
378.1'25—dc21   98-9787
                                                                                                                              CIP

Copy-edited and typeset by The Running Head Limited, London and Cambridge
Printed in Great Britain by St Edmundsbury Press Ltd, Bury St Edmunds, Suffolk

Contents

Preface – Why This Book Was Written

In 1986, after devoting 20 years to innovatory developments in open learning at Heriot-Watt University, I decided to seek the award of a higher doctorate for my work on Education for Capability (Cowan, 1986a). The usual practice is to submit a collection of publications for consideration by external examiners. But I was conscious that some of my papers had been written for educationists who preferred not to have to cope with matters of an engineering nature; and others had been written for engineers who weren't interested in the subtleties of educational theory or evaluation. So I took the option of writing a thesis – in which I tried to draw out the principles which had been the foundation of my practice, and the models to which I had been working. In so doing, I had the valuable opportunity to analyse my research and development, and to assemble a critical review of what I had done.

Shortly after that I moved to the Open University. I took charge of what amounted to a large multi-disciplinary educational unit, with particular concern for the development of personal and professional abilities by students who entered through an open access policy and who studied at a distance. Quickly I found myself building on the summary and review which my thesis had formulated, as I designed and presented new activities to meet the needs of these learners. I collaborated with a classicist, Judith George. We refined and extended my model for stimulating reflective learning. Because we were accommodated in adjacent rooms, we were able to work closely in planning and preparing – and evaluating. I profited enormously in my ten years with the Open University in having this working relationship with a colleague who shared my educational aspirations, is a facilitator of the highest order, and whose facilitation extended to the development of my own thinking and practice, through her keen questioning and critical comments.

Judith and I devoted a great deal of our effort to the creation of effective situations in which we worked with our tutorial colleagues on real problems and possibilities for their students. Especially we armed ourselves with tools of enquiry which tutors could use to discover – with their students – the nature of the students' immediate learning and of the learning experiences for which they, the tutors, were responsible. This in turn led us to pioneer workshops for staff and educational development which brought students and staff together in working towards real-life purposes (Cowan and George, 1993).

In the spring of 1994 I was invited to report on these developments (Cowan, 1995) at a European conference on Education for Science and Technology. I needed no persuasion to accept. I looked forward to the professional appraisal of my current work by participants whose values and interests I shared. In Stockholm, while renewing valued professional friendships, I made many new acquaintances. On the last day, as I contentedly prepared to return from what I was convinced had now been my last venture into this international arena, I was approached by Mona Dahms from Aalborg University. She suggested that we might work together, to progress in Denmark the ideas which I had piloted in Scotland. That we did, with what appear to be profitable outcomes for our students, our colleagues and ourselves. Mona provided the opportunity and the continued stimulus for me to move out and onwards once more, in search of new developments, new thinking and improved practice – and all of this at a time when I was a mere three years from retirement, and might not have sought new challenges on my own behalf. My debt to her is great, not least for the joy it has been to work with such an energetic teacher.

As the Aalborg initiative developed in parallel with what we were doing in Scotland, Mona decided that we should combine both staff and curriculum development in a substantial effort. This innovative and adventurous event was held at Slettestrand in North Jutland, and was literally a step forward into uncharted territory. I persuaded two of my part-time Scottish colleagues to join me as facilitators. Helen Wood had collaborated with me in the past, and in consequence had become a close friend as well as a kindred spirit. Claire Geddes had shared in some of the significant Scottish experiments of 1992–4. Neither had facilitated a major staff development workshop. At Slettestrand, we three – with the able cooperation of Mona – laid the foundations for subsequent developments at Aalborg, and much else besides. I cannot adequately thank the two Scots for trusting me in this venture, especially since I doubt if they fully appreciated at the time of my invitation the risk which acceptance entailed.

As well as my Open University duties and the Aalborg initiative, I also provided an annual workshop on reflection for the Aalborg course for university teachers, run by Anette Kolmos. She pointed out the need for a selection of backup papers on the place of reflection in higher education. I could not find anything suitable, and judged my own publications in need of an update as well as a linking commentary. Anette therefore suggested that I should write a short booklet, to be used at Aalborg and in the Open University. The existence of this text is due to her encouragement.

I showed my first rough draft pages for this booklet to Ray McAleese. He kindly enthused, and at the same time encouraged me to question myself more, in what was at that time my somewhat one-sided exposition. If this end result and its unusual layout prove useful and acceptable to you, we are both in Ray's debt for the helpful feedback he gave me on that early draft. But in consequence the short booklet grew until it became this wee book.

As I wrote, I sought feedback on various aspects of the draft from several friends, and profited from their constructive thoughts. None were more searching in their questioning of the underlying rationale than John Heywood and Elisabet Weedon. My correspondence with each has been, and continues to be, deep and thought-provoking. It has greatly enriched my thinking about reflective learning.

I hope this brief account of how I came to write this book has made it clear how much I am indebted to certain colleagues who have not always been easy to thank or acknowledge informally, face to face. I trust that it has also shown that we are ourselves reflective practitioners, following the practice and principles which we commend to our students, and continually developing our thinking in consequence.

John Cowan
January 1998

1

Introduction

On the structure of this text

I set out to write something practical on the topic of reflection in adult learning. I wanted to offer to my colleagues ideas which would be relevant to their work as ordinary teachers. I yearned to avoid the use of jargon and of specialized vocabulary which needs time to explain, to master and to assimilate. Since I have never wished to dwell on theories and pedagogies unless they are directly and almost immediately useful, I wanted to deal with theory or abstraction only as much as is necessary, and as succinctly as possible.

With these aspirations in mind, I decided to approach the chapters which follow in a somewhat unconventional style. I have:

- used questions to focus my inputs;
- given examples to answer these questions;
- generalized from the examples;
- used everyday language as much as possible.

That style and order were deliberately chosen. I ask you to bear with me for the next few pages, while I take each of these features in turn, and explain why I have judged them to be important.

Using questions to focus my inputs

In my work for the Open University, I concentrated on trying to help new students to become effective learners. In so doing, I set out to encourage these students to come to a way of studying in which they will notice questions which it will be worthwhile to ask. In addition, I tried to help them to formulate such questions in terms which – if posed to the right person – will generate answers which will be directly useful to them as learners, and will lead directly to progress, as far as their learning is concerned.

I am writing here for readers who, I presume, are themselves hoping to learn and develop as teachers. I wish to ensure that my text will be something which will help you directly. I would like to help you to advance in your understanding of what reflection in higher education can mean and achieve, and in your appreciation of how you can harness that potential, in your own situation and subject area. So I have chosen to avoid merely communicating information which matters to me, and which I want to pass on to you. Instead, I have done my best to identify or predict questions which could have been asked by the type of person for whom I believe I am writing. I have posed them starkly at the head of each chapter; and I have disciplined myself, as far as I am able, to keep the question at the front of my mind, as I was writing. I hope the questions I have chosen are ones with which you can identify.

Working from examples

Conceptual understanding generally begins from examples. Skemp, who was a mathematician turned educationist, argued this point with delightful effectiveness in a popular textbook (Skemp, 1971). He convinced me that, as a child, I was probably shown some things like a red car, a red book, a red pencil and a red traffic light – and hence acquired an understanding of the idea of 'red', which is a concrete concept. Then, sometime later, I would have encountered the abstract concept of 'colour', by being told, and by learning (again from examples), that red and blue and green are colours.

Skemp argued for the teaching of mathematics according to a similar approach. He believed that it is essential that a concept is first encountered in the form of examples which establish the beginnings of understanding. And he maintained that it is only when an initial understanding has been acquired, through the use and consideration of examples, that any abstract generalization or refinement of definition is then possible or meaningful. For only at that point, he asserted, has the learner developed sufficient understanding of the underlying concept on which to build theories and understanding which use and consolidate that concept.

In Berlin, in 1972, I attended an elegant demonstration of this approach – at an international conference on higher education. In her keynote address on the acquisition of concepts, Markle taught her audience, as she had taught her research subjects, the grammatical concept of a morpheme. First she provided an assortment of examples, all of which were undoubtedly morphemes – and so this concept was established in the minds of her listeners – including me, who had not hitherto encountered it. Then she quickly tabled a similar set of examples, all of which were not morphemes – although I might a little earlier have so classified them, while I was still somewhat uncertain about what a morpheme is. Thus the concept was yet more firmly concreted in the minds of the learners like me in the audience, as it had been in her research study. As her next step, and in refinement of our understanding, she gave us some borderline examples which were just morphemes and no more; and, finally, other borderline examples which were marginally not morphemes. By this point, we had well and truly mastered the concept of morpheme – from examples. Notice, of course, that the presenter had (and needed) a sound grasp of the concept, in order to make effective choices of examples. We, the learners, had not had any such understanding, until we worked with the examples as she arranged for us to do.

Conceptual understanding thus does indeed appear to begin from examples (of increasing subtlety) – although it is undoubtedly refined subsequently through the consideration and formulation of definitions, models, abstract approaches and theories. I would argue that, even in the case of fuzzy concepts which lack well-defined boundaries, we can only move towards the definitions from which we then define boundaries, when we have some idea – from examples – of the concept which we will then struggle to define, refining our understanding in so doing. In this text I have therefore answered each of the questions or tasks set for me by my imaginary reader, by presenting examples. If I have been successful, you will be able to establish your own personal understanding in your own way, and thence move towards your own generalizations and abstractions.

However, I am well aware that examples can be like anecdotes. If they are well chosen, they can have the seductive effect which most good anecdotes often have, which is to concentrate attention on the details of the story or example. They may then divert the reader, and the writer, from the underlying point or principle. I hope I have (nearly) avoided the danger of unhelpful digressions. I rely on you to remember that our aim is to make it possible for you to generalize from my examples, and so to be accordingly wary of my digressions.

Sometimes your generalizing will happen almost subconsciously, and in a distinctly personal and private way. But where situations and principles are rather more complex, and are more encumbered by additional and confusing detail, it is usually helpful if a teaching person prompts the process, and facilitates the explicit generalizing. In every chapter after this one, I have therefore followed each of my sets of examples with some thoughts of my own, pointing towards tentative and partly formed generalizations, which I leave you to revise, to redraft or to compose anew – in your own way and for yourself. Learners differ; so learning should never be regarded as a one-way street – for where there is one way, there must, almost by definition, be another way or perhaps quite a few other ways. You will explore some of these for yourself, I hope, as we progress through my examples.

In adopting a facilitative style, I admit that I seek to do more than nurture your conceptual understanding of reflective learning. I will also use examples to offer you models and ideas for you to test, by applying these in turn to further examples which will emerge from your own activity, and will be personal to you and to your students.

Until we reach Chapter 11, you will find that most of my examples are taken from my own first-hand experience, and are therefore inevitably drawn from my activities in Heriot-Watt University and the Open University. I have chosen to restrict my coverage in this way because I do not wish to write much about second-hand experience, which would entail interpreting someone else's work and their reflective self-evaluation.

I will attempt to redress that imbalance in Chapter 11. But I do so with grudging acceptance of a commonly expressed need which troubles me. For, as I will argue in Chapter 8, perhaps too much is made, in Britain especially, of the alleged distinctness of our disciplines, which some would claim are so fundamentally different that we cannot learn much from educational practice outside our own area. That has not been my experience, either when I have been pillaging good ideas from another subject, and eagerly transferring them with good effect into my own learning and teaching; or when I have moved, as a student and learner, from engineering to theology, and then to education, and so to social sciences. I have certainly found that disciplines vary in the emphasis which they place on the cognitive and affective abilities demanded of the learner, but not in the general nature or relevance of these abilities. That is one reason why I do all that I can to develop interdisciplinary abilities which will prove profitable to the learner, whatever the next subject of study proves to be. Similarly, as a teacher, I value interdisciplinary transfer and the transferability of good ideas for teaching and learning.

I therefore ask you to suspend disbelief on this matter of disciplinary constraints, at least until we have considered it further in Chapter 8. You will then be in a position to decide if significant interdisciplinary differences are a valid obstacle to transfer – or are merely perhaps a frequently quoted form of defence against a perceived challenge from more developed practice elsewhere.

Nevertheless, one matter troubles me about my concentration on the use of examples, and that is their discrete nature. I appreciate that transforming your teaching process is a long and gradual task, which is usually done incrementally. It is probable and natural that you will want to begin tentatively, by using individual ideas in a compartmentalized way, and then will gradually extend your appreciation of the essence of them into a complete process. However, there is a risk in taking up isolated examples for which the new context is inappropriate. I caution you that it may prove dangerous if you simply insert into your curricula the strategies which I describe – as individual exercises. They may not sit comfortably with the status quo, and the disharmony may be positively unhelpful to you and your students.

Using everyday language

Researchers have studied adventurers who have sailed solo around the world. These hardy souls have apparently worried on occasions for their mental health because, when acute trouble was at hand, they began to talk to themselves. They are greatly reassured, I am told, to learn that people who talk to themselves at times of trial tend to be more effective in their problem-solving than they would have been if they had not done so. This finding is certainly consistent with my own modest experience some 20 years ago, when I researched the problem-solving activities of my students, in distinctly less spectacular or demanding circumstances (Cowan, 1977, 1980a).

I had persuaded some of my undergraduates to talk out their thoughts aloud, as they solved the type of problems which confronted them in their studies with me as their teacher. These reports, or recorded protocols if we use the proper vocabulary, were transcribed, so that I could analyse and use my findings about learning difficulties as a basis for curriculum development (Example 9.1). As my research enquiry progressed, I was surprised but pleased to discover that these students were becoming more effective problem-solvers, in this and in other subjects. So talking out your thoughts aloud, and thinking about what that revealed, seemed to be profitable for my students as well as for their teacher. (The same is true, in my experience, when you write down a reflective account of your thoughts in what has come to be called a learning journal, as described in Example 2.3 – but I suspect there are important differences between the slow reflective nature of writing, and the speedier act of talking.)

In my recorded protocol studies I found that the language which the students used to describe their problem-solving was more colloquial than that in which they wrote when they were drafting coursework for submission, or when they were writing examination papers. This language of their running commentaries was also more colloquial than the language they used in talking to me, when they asked me for help or tried to tell me what they were doing in their problem-solving. (In all of this, I admit difficulty in handling the recorded exclamations and bad language, to which most students regressed when things went wrong – and which told yet another story.)

A friend recently provided for me a delightful example of the fact that we often use shared colloquial language to express our personal version of disciplinary thinking. He instanced a teacher who deliberately employed this ploy, when bringing out the importance of the sensuous and evocative specificity of good literary writing. He would begin his first year tutorials with a comparison of two passages describing an island – one perhaps from Ballantyne's *Coral Island* and the other from William Golding's *Lord of the Flies*. He would get the students to see that one description was vague and generalized, whereas the other made one feel that the writer had actually been there, and had seen things for himself. After that, this teacher would often activate and then test this critical criterion, which he then generalized, by colloquially and yet meaningfully asking the students, of some quite different piece of writing, 'Has this author been on the island?'

I suggest to you that we only use the more formal language of our discipline when we communicate punctiliously with others, or record our professional thoughts on paper. Otherwise we do much of our personal professional thinking in colloquial language. That is my reason for trying, initially, to avoid using words which do not already have meaning for you, or for others of my readers. To be sure, as we progress from my examples and from your understanding to our generalizations and abstractions, we will undoubtedly need to make, or will at least profit from, some use of a specialized and generally accepted vocabulary which will cover new depths of appreciation, or allow us to make subtle distinctions. This will especially be the case when we wish to explain our thinking to others, or to specify something with precision. It will also be helpful, as we progress, if we employ (and are therefore first introduced to), words which are commonly used educationally, and have a special meaning in that context. But in these pages I have earnestly tried to delay the use of specialized vocabulary for as long as possible. For I am sure that it is in our own language that we first think about any personal learning which really matters to us. And my commitment to that belief appears so far to have paid off for me, and for my students.

I hope I have already begun in a language which we can share and in which we should be able to find shared meanings. I will continue to write as plainly as I can, in what follows.

Summary

For the reasons I have explained, I have decided that I will present the content of this book in a series of chapters, having the following structure:

- I will begin with a *question*, written as if addressed to me by you, the reader, or by other teachers who have asked me over the years about this business of reflection in the education of adults.
- I will next attempt to give a response to that question, within a number of distinct *examples*.
- After each sequence of examples, I will add a *generalization* or two, to prompt (but not, I trust, to direct) the process of assimilation on your part.
- Thereafter, to ensure that I do not have things all my own way, I will generally attempt to prompt your *second thoughts*, by offering an alternative view or posing valid questions on which you may wish to ponder, as you consider testing out, in your own context, what you can take from my examples and your generalizations.

In the next chapter I set out to help you to an understanding, shared with me, of what reflection in higher education entails. We will then move on to consider what reflection has to offer in the education of adults, and in particular how it helps when we aspire to develop cognitive and interpersonal abilities. After that, we will consider what you and I can do as teachers to encourage our students to reflect effectively – and the differences in emphasis between reflection which is predominantly analytical and reflection which is mainly evaluative. If the facilitation of reflective learning then seems worthwhile to you, I imagine you will then welcome some help about how to get started, and after that some ideas for evaluation of your efforts as an innovative teacher. Finally, in a book based heavily on the experience of one man and his immediate colleagues, we'll take a look at what others have been doing.

Let's begin, then, almost without further ado, with a thought to prompt your immediate reflection about the topic which brings us together. Pierre Teilhard de Chardin, in *The Phenomenon of Man* (1955: 165), suggested that

Reflection is . . . the power acquired by a consciousness to turn in upon itself, to take possession of itself as an object endowed by its own particular consistence and value; no longer merely to know, but to know one's self; no longer merely to know, but to know that one knows . . .

Dear John

I know, of course, what the word 'reflection' means, in everyday situations. But I can't see why this activity should be singled out nowadays for special attention in further and higher education.

I've always thought of education, and especially higher education, in terms of my own experience as a student. In my undergraduate days, I had teachers who taught me what I had to learn, according to a syllabus. Then I went off and tried to master that learning, so that I could demonstrate that I could use it – in the coursework which they set for me, and in the examinations which I had to pass.

While I was busy with all of that, I wasn't conscious of doing much in the way of detached reflection. To be frank, I don't think there was time for thinking about what I was doing. I had to concentrate on getting on with what had to be done. I had to try to do it well, if I wanted to score good marks and gain a degree of the best possible standard. That worked out all right for me. So it cannot really have been too inadequate, can it?

I'm wondering why this business of reflection is being given so much attention nowadays in education. What is it? What does it lead to, which wouldn't happen without reflection? And, if my students are expected to reflect, what does that demand of me, in my case as a university teacher?

John, I know you cannot possibly answer all my questions at once. So can you please start me off at the beginning by simply giving me some understanding of what is meant in education nowadays when they speak of 'reflection'.

2

What is Meant in Education by 'Reflecting'?

Introduction

I hope it will be helpful if I briefly outline the structure of this chapter, before you begin to read it.

I'll keep the question at the head of this chapter firmly in mind as I write. I'll begin by giving four examples of reflection in higher education, taken from four different contexts and subject areas. In each example I'll finish by identifying those parts of the activity which called on students to reflect. To help you to tune your use of the word to mine, I'll then offer a few further one-line examples of reflection, followed by several non-examples.

After that, I will offer you my own generalization about what reflection means to and for me, when I am learning in ways which depend on reflection. And then, as I promised, I'll close with second thoughts on this whole matter – expressed from the standpoint of someone who might critically appraise what I have written in the preceding pages.

Example 2.1: Reflecting on dealing effectively with obstacles to your learning

If isolated students in the Open University (OU) are to survive and prosper academically in their post-foundation studies, they must learn, one way or another, to be somewhat self-sufficient. Such self-sufficiency calls for the development of study skills which go well beyond the making of notes, or preparing to write an essay, or even the routine application of the content which is presented in the published study units.

Some years ago I collaborated with Judith George, who was at that time responsible for the academic care of the students in the sparsely populated south of Scotland. We designed and presented a skills programme at the OU's Dumfries study centre (Cowan and George, 1989). The activities in our programme were planned to help the students in an interdisciplinary group, determined by geography, to develop what we described as survival and developmental skills. For reasons which I hope will become apparent, we began to tackle a new skill in the middle of our activity for a particular evening; and we finished dealing with it in the middle of our next evening with the students, which occurred some four or five weeks later.

We began with our choice of a skills area which we expected to be judged relevant by the students. For example, we chose for one workshop 'Overcoming study difficulties, when you're on your own'. We began in that case by getting the students to make up their own personal lists of obstacles which they had already encountered in their learning, and which had thwarted their progress. In their groups of four or five, they began by swapping experiences. For example, one of them had had great trouble working out what to concentrate on in the second block of the social sciences foundation course. Another had disagreed with something in the materials for a Third World course, and wasn't sure what to do about it.

After the initial exchange of particular experiences within each group, we encouraged the students to try to 'pigeonhole' these obstacles metaphorically, under headings or titles which were meaningful to them, and which could include several examples under one heading. The first problem I mentioned above went with others under 'How can I tell the difference between need to know and nice to know?' The second figured as 'What if I think the materials say something wrong?'

The entire group of 20–25 students now worked together with a tutor as their facilitator, and were eventually able to reach a fair degree of agreement about titles for the various categories of obstacles which had been experienced by one or more in the entire group. These were listed by the tutor on a flipchart.

We next set the small groups the task of examining their experiences with obstacles of each of the types listed on the flipchart. We asked them to recall occasions in the past where, at some time, at least one of them had been successful in overcoming that type of blockage to their learning. And we got them to summarize what these solutions had entailed, again remaining with particular examples for as long as possible in that process.

The groups now reported back, in plenary, and were assisted as before by the tutor who was acting as their scribe. She took a generalized problem title, often still in colloquial terms and always using the students' words, from the flipchart sheet. As one group or another suggested ways in which that type of obstacle might be overcome, the scribe summarized that method, at first orally and in particular terms, but then more briefly and in generalized terms. She still took care to use the students' vocabulary, but wherever possible cleverly tried to omit detail which related only to one particular circumstance. For example, in the 'need to know/nice to know' area, she helped the group to the terse and shared advice: 'Find out what they want in assignments and exams – because that's need to know'.

Even after prolonged group discussion and exploration, the workshop might fail to come up with an effective solution to a really difficult problem. In that case, a tutor might intervene with a suggestion. This occurred rarely – and with reluctance on the part of the tutors. When this happened the students were immediately charged to appraise the feasibility of the suggestion, according to their experiences as contained in the examples which they had used to describe the obstacle; and then they had to decide whether or not to take the suggested tactic on board.

And so it was that, by the end of the second half of that first evening, the plenary group had prepared, virtually on their own, what amounted to their advice to themselves, when faced with obstacles to their independent learning. This statement set out a summary of the types of obstacle they might expect to encounter in their studies, and (more importantly) related these to a constructive and generalized summary of their own ideas about how each of these obstacles might best be tackled. This advice, which was now expressed only in general terms, was word-processed for the students on the next working day, and immediately posted out to them.

During the next three or four weeks, the students, virtually in isolation, continued with their studies. When they encountered further obstacles in that learning, they were encouraged to attempt to use the generalized advice which they had generated for themselves. Sometimes they were successful in overcoming the obstacles they met; sometimes they were unsuccessful; sometimes they discovered in their struggles how to enrich the advice on the summary sheet; and sometimes they discovered that it was oversimplified, and needed to be refined. Time, and repeated returning to the generalizations in hand, enhanced their appreciation of the potential of their self-generated advice, and their ability to improve on it.

When the group came together again, with the benefit of the intervening period of practical experience, the students exchanged their accounts of what they had been doing. Some reported successes, and extensions to the group's methodology; and, when they did so (through anecdotal examples), many of the others were able to profit accordingly. Some students reported frustrations, and were assisted by others to see how these might have been overcome – again enhancing the general methodology.

The first part of that second evening was structured so that, from consideration of examples taken from their recent study experiences, the students worked to improve their own advice to themselves – in this case advice about how to deal with obstacles to their learning. As they did this, they were now in a sense amending the word-processed sheets which had been sent out. But they hardly needed these sheets any more – because the methodology had virtually become an integral part of their ways of working, and of their thinking.

We could then move on to a different topic, and tackle it within much the same structure. It might be 'How can you assemble a sound argument, or proof?' or 'How can you score more marks in assignments and examinations, without working any harder or having brain surgery?' Once a topic had been agreed as worthwhile, we could set off again in the now familiar pattern of reflective and constructive group and individual working.

On the first half-evening devoted to this type of activity, these students were reflecting when they

- categorized the types of obstacles they had encountered in their learning;
- identified in general terms how such obstacles might be overcome;
- summarized their advisory methodology in general terms.

During the interim five weeks, and in the half-meeting which followed, the students were also reflecting when, having tested out their generalized advice in new situations, they either confirmed that it worked, or decided that it needed to be refined or that it had to be extended. Notice that the scheduling of two half-evenings to the one topic, with learning experiences intervening, contributed to the integration with real-life demands which is often lacking, but pedagogically desirable, in developmental learning activities.

Example 2.2: Reflecting on families of problems

In teaching applied mechanics to a first year class, I would produce a worksheet of problems which all seemed to me to belong to the one 'family'. Every student in the class would be given a photocopy of this worksheet. I would display another copy, on an acetate, using the overhead projector. I would now stand with my back to the screen, in such a position that I obviously could not see what was displayed there. I would invite a student to come out from the class, and – silently – indicate one of the problems on the sheet which that student wished us to try to solve. From my position, I couldn't tell which example had been chosen.

This student then worked on a second overhead projector, according to instructions which I would call out. There was no dialogue between myself and the student, other than occasional and simple questions from me which the student could answer in a monosyllable. I sometimes merely needed the student to tell me which branch in the developing sequence of steps I was taking him or her down. Otherwise the student did as I said, and was charged to display no initiative. The other students were asked to check that this was so. In four cases out of five, the student at the front would either solve the problem by following my (virtually blindfold) instructions; if this student had difficulty, another could readily be persuaded to come out from the class, and would usually be able to follow the instructions – which I did not change.

Once the problem had been solved, I displayed my method for the first time on the overhead projector, as a general outline which could be applied to all problems in the family contained on the worksheet. I would have called that an algorithm, were I in the company of other teachers of this subject. But when I talked to the students, I didn't describe what was on my acetate as an algorithm. I just used everyday words and explained 'Here's what I was trying to get your classmate to do on my behalf'. I was now demonstrating to the class what I meant by a standardized method for solving that family of problems – leaving each student to think of the contents of my acetate under whatever title seemed appropriate to them.

My real goal was to help the students to develop the ability to derive their own algorithm, or whatever they would call it, for another family of problems with which they already had some acquaintance. And so I now gave them all, in groups of four or five, a second worksheet containing problems in that new family, based on another approach or principle. I asked them each to take a different problem from that sheet, and try to solve it, and then think about how they had been doing it. This task took them some time to complete.

With this experience behind them, I asked them as a group to 'produce an acetate like mine' for this second family of problems. Their acetate should give a precise method of solution which would apply to all of the problems on the second sheet, as universally as mine had proved applicable to all of the problems on the first sheet. Later they tested their acetate and its instructions with a student from another group.

These students were reflecting on how they had solved their individual problems when they each thought about the method they had used in solving them; they were reflecting when they tried to communicate that analysis to each other, in general terms. They were also reflecting, in a group, about the formulation of a basic method which could be used for all the problems on the sheet, when they tried to produce an acetate for the second family of problems, like the one I had shown them for the first family. Their various reflections involved thinking about how they had been doing it, where 'doing it' could be the method which they used for one example – or for several examples, which made up a 'family'.

Example 2.3: Reflecting on 'unpicking log-jams'

(This example makes an interesting contrast with the first one. I'll refer to that contrast in my 'second thoughts', at the end of this chapter.)

In the early 1980s, my first year students in Heriot-Watt University studied a course called Interdisciplinary Studies. Three timetabled hours per week had been found for this course, by reducing the allocation of hours which was given to civil engineering subjects from 15 hours per week to 12 hours per week. The remaining nine hours per week were devoted to mathematics, physics and chemistry.

Interdisciplinary Studies, titled 'IDS' by the students, set out unashamedly to develop abilities which really matter in studies in higher education, and in professional life. Roughly speaking, the first term of the three-term course concentrated mainly on communication in the broadest sense of that word, including the abilities of listening, empathizing with feelings, and so on. The second term concentrated mainly on problem-solving, again in the most liberal sense of that title. And the third dwelt on relevant aspects of interpersonal skills, since much of the first year course programme in my department depended on a wide range of group activities and project work.

A powerful component in the learning and teaching situation which had been set up for this course was the weekly writing and submitting for comment of what we called 'learning journals'. The purpose of the journal was to require the student to think carefully about the answer to some such question as 'What have I learned about learning or thought about thinking, as a result of these IDS activities, which should make me more effective next week than I was last week?' Students were encouraged, if they so wished, to rephrase that question, to define 'effective' in their own terms, and to focus their reflective journal writing – all as they found most useful.

Each learning journal was read either by me or by my colleague, Derek Fordyce. We told the students that we knew in broad outline what they had done in our class that week – as well as, or better than, they themselves did. Consequently, or so we conveniently and emphatically told them, they should avoid recording events – for only thus could they ensure that this would be a reflective journal which concentrated on thinking about thinking, rather than a diary devoted to factual detail.

It was a coursework requirement that learning journals had to be submitted each week. Initially the students had great difficulty with that demand – because it was a strange and abstract one, calling on them to engage in an unfamiliar activity. Perhaps there was a growing awareness of the usefulness of the tutors' comments, and appreciation of the confidentiality of the process which never called for any conversation with the tutor, although this might happen if (rarely) the student so wished. We were also helped by the the presence on campus of second year students, some of whom continued to keep journals after it was no longer a requirement. They could testify sincerely to the eventual impact of the activity on their learning abilities.

The journals came in for comment each Thursday morning. As quickly as possible, Derek and I commented on them, without offering any judgements or even suggesting where and how to improve. We simply tried to understand and to identify with what was written. Where we didn't understand, we asked a question – but it was not a threatening or critical question, simply a question genuinely suggesting the need to clarify. Where there seemed to be a break in the logic, we gently pointed it out, but without implying criticism or suggesting how the break might be repaired. Where it would have been helpful to test a confident statement against recent experience, we suggested how that might be done, without implying that it should be done. Where a success was reported, we enthused. We expected no response to come to us. There was seldom any feedback of that type.

If Derek and I worked hard, the journals could be back in the students' pigeon-holes on the Friday morning. If so then, in an astonishing rush, the journals would disappear in about six minutes flat – with students standing around in the lounge area a few metres away, eagerly reading our comments which they virtually never discussed with the staff who had provided them, and which they never appeared to discuss with their fellow students. That behaviour suggested to us that the activity, and the comments, were valued – which does not necessarily mean they were valuable.

The students struggled with this strange need to write – and to think – reflectively. A typical journal, in the beginning, tended to contain a halting entry which was seldom more than half a page long. But, by the middle of the second term, it was not uncommon for someone who had had a 'blue flash' or a Damascus Road experience, to wish to write for us at length, sometimes up to ten pages (see also Example 10.8).

Now, to the IDS programme itself. What happened in a typical week? I begin my detailed description at the end of the previous week, and from a journal entry.

During the second term, a student had volunteered in his reflective learning journal that he had had considerable success as a result of the previous week's activity in IDS, which had been devoted to developing a general problem-solving approach for use in numerate subject areas:

It was great. I went to my physics problem class the following day. For the first time since I came here, I found I could answer the first three questions on the sheet without help. And I got the correct answers. I moved on to question four. I didn't get the correct answer – but as soon as I looked at the answer on the sheet, I could see where I had gone wrong.

Then I tried question five, and I didn't know where to start. I looked at my lecture notes, and I couldn't find anything to help me; but I couldn't find anything in the lecture notes that I didn't understand, either. I looked at the set book. I couldn't find anything there to help me. And, again, I couldn't find anything which appeared to be relevant, and which I didn't understand.

So I had a log-jam in my problem-solving. It was stuck and wouldn't move. I don't want anyone to show me how to answer question 5. I want someone to help me to unpick log-jams.

I spoke to the class, and told them the substance of this account – without identifying the person who had written it. I asked how many others had encountered a 'log-jam' situation in their recent studies. Some two-thirds of them identified with the experience, and admitted that it had baffled them; they could only attempt to overcome it by seeking help with the particular problem in which their problem-solving had been thwarted at the outset. They quoted examples, with which some other students in the class identified. This led us almost immediately to a negotiated and precise meaning for the colloquial title which the original student had coined, which then had that meaning for this class during the remainder of that year.

Derek and I undertook to prepare a response to this declared need. We devised a workshop activity accordingly. During the two hours which were timetabled for the class on the Tuesday afternoon, we arranged for the students to explore and analyse successful and unsuccessful methods of unpicking log-jams, taken from their, and our, experiences. After this structured sequence of activities, each group of students charted their progress, and their outstanding difficulties, on flipchart sheets. They left these for us, in the working area, as informative wallpaper; and after that they went off happily (I hope), either to their home or to their hall of residence.

Derek and I looked at the flipchart sheets, identified the progress (and lack of progress) which the groups had made, and reconsidered the activity which we had scheduled, as a form of learning enhancement and consolidation, for the first hour on the Wednesday morning. (In running IDS, we sometimes found that our tentative plans for that follow-on hour had to be radically changed. On this occasion, as I recall it, they only had to be mildly modified.)

On the Wednesday morning, we facilitated a one-hour activity in which the groups tested out a further (constructive) input from us, which incorporated much that they had assembled in their summaries of the previous afternoon. After that, the students went back into their other classes. And on the Wednesday evening, following these experiences of the Tuesday and of the entire Wednesday, they wrote the next entries in their reflective learning journals.

It was from one such (earlier) journal entry that I had extracted the suggestion that dealing with log-jams might be useful, in the following week.

These students were reflecting when they

- analysed past experiences during the workshop activity in groups on the Tuesday afternoon, and attempted to generalize from that;
- tried to consolidate and extend the total group experience along similar lines, during the Wednesday morning activity;
- individually related the IDS activity to their learning experiences in the remainder of the Wednesday, and brought that together in a critical and analytical journal entry;
- individually thought forward to their forthcoming needs, and ruminated on these privately in their journals.

Example 2.4: Aalborg University's Basic Education Year, for technology students

In the aftermath of the students' revolts of 1968, a number of universities in northern Europe established courses based on project orientation. These are unlike the traditional British programme in which a project, when it figures in the curriculum, is an extended exercise based on the taught syllabus. The project in project-orientation is the origin of learning and teaching; for the students only study that which they need to master, in order to cope with the demands of the problem at the heart of their project.

The current Basic Education Year, for students of technology at Aalborg University (formerly Aalborg University Centre) is a modified example of project-oriented study of this form. Students arrive at the university either directly from school or, more commonly, after a gap year between school and university. They enter a Basic Education Year in which half of their time will be spent in groups working on projects; a quarter will be given to project-unit courses, in which the subject matter arises from their learning needs as occasioned by the project. The remaining time is devoted to study-unit courses, in areas such as computing and physics, where it is apparent to all concerned that instruction will be needed by all students, and that there is no point in playing a game of learner-directed learning for this part of the syllabus.

Group working is central to all of this, and communication skills and reflection on learning are demanded in assessment and elsewhere. Project groups have two supervisors, one of whom – the main and technical supervisor – is responsible for the technical content of the project and for the development and assessment of process competencies. The other (assistant) supervisor, who is usually a social scientist, is charged to ensure that the group take due account of the social implications of both their problem and their suggested solution.

The Aalborg academic year is divided into two semesters, but the project timings in the Basic Education Year subdivide that period still further. For the study year begins with the P0 project, which is in some ways an exploratory and a 'throw-away' experience. It is a mini-project of only four weeks' duration, intended to give students a taste of what lies ahead. At the end of this non-assessed experience, the students have an opportunity to pause and reflect on what it has meant, and implies, for them. They do this in a residential event, which is led by students from later years of the course. At this time they mull over what they have done, and what they will have to do in a full project. And then they return to university, to begin the slightly curtailed P1 project, which runs for the remainder of the first semester. The P1 project is an assessed part of their studies.

A project originates in a problem area. One such problem area, which was explored recently by a full class group (*ca.* 100 students) was the matter of working conditions in industry in Aalborg. Project groups (of five or six students) identified problems within that problem area. One group chose to concentrate on the noise levels in the butcheries; another on the fact that EC regulations will shortly render mushroom growing, as practised in Denmark, illegal – and hence will lead to the demise of the mushroom growing industry unless a way can be found to improve working conditions. Consequently the butchery group found that they needed study-unit courses on acoustics, while the group concerned on behalf of the mushroom growers required instruction in biology, and the effect of spores and the like on human beings.

The project is assessed under two headings. One is the success of the group in tackling the problem which they formulated. The other begins from the group's review of their performance. They should present a realistic and analytical self-appraisal of the processes they followed, and a constructive identification of their learning needs and their aspirations for the project they will undertake, perhaps in different groups, in the second semester. Supervisors nowadays make a strong input to the process analysis between the P1 project and the P2 project, and facilitate a one-day session in which attention is concentrated on the review and assessment by the students of their progress and processes. For this Aalborg Basic Education Year, as it is currently presented, stresses critical self-appraisal of that which is past or current, leading into a constructive preparation for the challenge of that which is yet to come. The demand of process analysis which the team of supervisors has introduced clearly places considerable formal emphasis on explicit reflection about what the students have done or are doing as a group, how they can improve on that, and on what they should concentrate, next time round.

These students are reflecting frequently throughout their Basic Education Year, when they are discussing, planning and evaluating how they do things (as occasioned by individual situations within the project groups) and when – between and after projects – they respond to the requirements of review, assessment and forward planning.

Other examples

- A student is reflecting when she notes that there is something different about the case that she is considering, in comparison with the examples she has encountered in class; and when she also identifies what the difference is, and what she should do about it.

- A golfer is reflecting when he notices that, in certain circumstances, five out of six shots curl away to the right – and when he wonders what the correlation may be between that type of shot, and that type of deflection.
- A student is reflecting when she reads the comments on an assignment, and tries to deduce from them some guidelines which can help her produce better work in the next assignment in that discipline, which will be on a different topic.
- A student is reflecting when he looks back on a plan which was not as successful as he had hoped, and tries to identify what it was that he did not anticipate, and how that knowledge should affect his planning for a future but similar occasion.
- A car driver is reflecting when she begins to assemble a mental list of behaviours by other drivers, which signal that she might well anticipate unpredictable actions on their part, when they are near her on the road.

Non-examples

In contrast:

- A student is not reflecting when he rephrases an explanation which has been given to him, and passes it on to a fellow student.
- A student is not reflecting when she merely narrates to herself what she did.
- A student is not reflecting when he regurgitates the perceptive views of his teacher or of the writer of a recommended textbook.

Generalization

One way of answering the question which is at the head of this chapter would be to maintain that learners are reflecting, in an educational sense, when they analyse or evaluate one or more personal experiences, and attempt to generalize from that thinking. They do this so that, in the future, they will be more skilful or better informed or more effective, than they have been in the past.

When I searched my experience for examples to illustrate reflection, and went on to ruminate about the common features which they might all share – and which would define what reflection entails – then I was myself reflecting analytically. When I compared Examples 2.1 (the OU skills sessions) and 2.3 (the Heriot-Watt IDS programme), and made up my mind with precision and clarity about the pedagogic effectiveness of each and what that suggests to me for the next time I set out to help similar learners face learning difficulties, I was reflecting evaluatively as well as analytically.

Reflection often involves me in thinking about how I did something – which is analytical. It can also involve me in thinking about how well I have done something – which is evaluative. (Remember that distinction, please; I will want to develop it later on, in Chapters 6 and 7.) I picture analytical reflection as being rather like a bridge between particular experiences and generalizations, or as the shared area where theory overlaps with practice. It begins in situations where

I have thought hard about one or more experiences. Through reflection, I can formulate a generalization which attempts to bring together and summarize all that is evident and relevant in the examples, and which may usefully inform my action, in future similar experiences. I picture evaluative reflection as a matching or mismatching of my performance and my aspirations, with the intention to minimize that gap, by learning from my mistakes, failures – and successes.

You may well be wondering already what my detailed generalizations are with regard to this business of reflection in learning. Since I would rather that you formulated your own generalizations, I will now simply try to facilitate your reflection on that task, with my second thoughts on this matter, as promised.

Some second thoughts

I have a distinct advantage in this text. For it is I who control the input, and direct the thinking. At this point, it is therefore only fair to offer an opportunity for you to look at this first input of mine from a different standpoint. Some second thoughts, then:

1. I seem to have concentrated on reflection as a distinct activity. Would it not be more accurate to portray reflection as an adjunct to experiencing, which happens even as you experience?
2. Are there really sound reasons for treating reflection as something which happens because we stand outside ourselves and our actions? If so, is it always to be separate, or usually so – or simply sometimes so?
3. Examples 2.1 (OU) and 2.3 (Heriot-Watt) are rather similar; but you will have noted that in Example 2.3 inputs were more generously supplied by the tutors than in Example 2.1. Should tutors contribute in this way, rather than facilitate? Or should they strive to restrict themselves to facilitation of reflection?
4. Surely thoughtful students from time immemorial have been reflecting almost as described here, without the intervention and structuring of zealous teachers. Is the stress on reflection anything more than a remedial operation to cater for students who should be able to engage in this aspect of learning and development, but cannot do so on their own, as their predecessors did in the past?

My own reflections on my reflecting

Apart from reflection which I would describe as incidental, I know that I myself reflect deliberately when:

- I have *committed myself* to reflect, and know how and when I intend to prompt myself to do so.
- I *notice something* which perturbs me, and I reflect in order to find improvement, explanation or understanding.
- I am *asked a question* which I cannot answer without reflecting; or I am given a task which makes a similar demand.

- An *intervention* by someone, not necessarily my tutor, requires me to think reflectively.
- *Dialogue* with a peer prompts me to engage in reflection, which may be shared.
- *I decide that I should reflect* on my processes of reflection, and determine my own outcomes and my desired standards in that reflection about reflection.

I assembled that list carefully. I used the words in italics to describe the occasions which most commonly prompt me to reflect. I then chose the order of items so that it illustrates the level of difficulty, for me. The demand increases for me as I make my way downwards. Similarly, the intellectual reward appears to grow with the demand, and is greater for me in the instances towards the foot of my list.

I see a meaningful relationship in my case between the different types of event which occasion reflection on my part, the nature of my consequent reflection process, and the type of outcome which I can expect from it. But is that relationship significant and reliable, or is it just wishful thinking on my part to rationalize in this way?

I still have a long way to go before I am ready to answer that last question. But I find it useful to revisit it from time to time; and I use it to take my thinking a little step further forward. It certainly makes me think harder about the activities I plan for my students, when I hope to encourage them to reflect. Perhaps my question is something on which you, too, will wish to ponder, for that reason.

Dear John

Maybe I'm just out of touch with what's happening in the more progressive parts of higher education. But it seems to me that you've chosen to begin with some rather unusual examples. As a result, although I'm quite intrigued by what you've written, I find I've been more interested so far in the ways in which you are teaching, than in the need to incorporate reflection as a feature in my own teaching and learning situations.

I'd still like to know a bit more about why you feel that this reflection business is needed. What's wrong with the way higher education was before, at least when it was well presented? Surely the traditional seminar is set up to occasion reflection? Have there not always been forms of teaching which have challenged students to do their own thinking about the content of what they were learning, in ways akin to the examples you've just given me in that last chapter?

You've mentioned the contribution which you think reflection makes to the development of abilities. Do you not acknowledge that abilities have always mattered a great deal in all vocational education, from education for the ministry to education for engineering, medicine and surgery? We graduates of a previous era developed our abilities fairly well under the old regime. Your own education, for instance, appears to have produced a thinking, creative and successful graduate. And, if it did that, it can't have been all that wrong in its methodology, I conclude.

So why do you feel the need to put so much explicit stress on reflection in your teaching nowadays? What does reflection have to offer?

3

What Does Reflection Have to Offer in Education?

Introduction

In this chapter, I'll offer six examples to suggest that reflection has something to offer education. The first three examples describe situations in which the advent of IT has made reflection possible, and effective for worthwhile learning. The next two set out the case and the demand for educational outcomes which are best achieved through the use of reflection; and the last example describes an institution in which that demand has been anticipated, and met in a manner which has attracted attention and praise. After that you'll find further examples and non-examples to suggest that reflection does, and may not, have something to offer. Then, after some tentative generalizations from me, I'll finish with a quartet of serious caveats to stimulate your second thoughts on the questions which have been raised, and the answers which I have given.

Example 3.1: New technologies promote reflection – in mathematics

Some years ago, the Open University foundation course in mathematics contained an activity which dealt with topics drawn from the study of calculus. This occupied one half-day of the one-week long residential summer school programme, which is also described in Example 5.5. The activity was designed, primarily, as revision and consolidation. It took the students over familiar ground, bringing together one or two topics in a fresh way. But it offered no new teaching, for revision and remedial tuition were the main objectives. However, in an attempt to make the subject matter and the challenge a little more rewarding, the tasks for small groups were shaped so that they pointed forward to a short and potentially interesting closing lecture. In this, the learners could be shown that what they had been doing, as first year students, could lead on into the development of the relatively new and complex concept of mathematical chaos. The lecturer was briefed to demonstrate this complex theme, but was fortunate (and extremely competent) if the resultant lecture even managed to convince the students that what they had been doing was reasonably worthwhile. As a tutor in attendance at the time, I cannot recall ever forming the impression that the students in these classes had grasped the concept of chaos – nor did I feel any criticism of the lecturers for failing to achieve that outcome.

Six years on from my first encounter with this summer school activity, the OU was able to introduce computers to the groupwork in this part of the programme. Students were provided with some elementary software, and an ingenious adaptation of an otherwise standard spreadsheet. This software enabled them to explore questions in the form 'What would happen if . . .?' They were encouraged, but not directed, to explore what would happen if there were changes in the magnitudes of the populations of rabbits and predatory foxes, or of their habits, in an island area with limited potential for the vegetation to grow. The students had met the software a few days before, and were reasonably familiar with it. They were able to use it to investigate in a short time many possibilities which they generated in their own ways; and they could thus engage almost automatically in creative reflection spurred by their curiosity. This led them to deeply perceptive generalizations, which they could then test out and further develop in study of new examples.

After a mere hour spent in exploring the potential of the learning materials to enable them to discover 'What would happen if . . .', most of those in the groups which I happened to be tutoring that year had begun to discover for themselves the main features of this complex concept of mathematical chaos. Yet this was the concept which lecturers in previous years had struggled in vain to convey in the lecture format, which had been generously supported by excellent audio-visual aids and computerized displays. The availability and structured use of software for direct student engagement in open learning had made it a straightforward reality to achieve speedily, through self-directed reflection, the mastery of a concept which had never before been seriously contemplated as a possible learning outcome.

Example 3.2: New technologies promote reflection – in economics

I was involved in facilitating a Teaching Quality Improvement Scheme at Salford University. In one project, we enabled a lecturer teaching business economics to purchase access to a massive data bank which had been prepared for commercial and not instructional purposes. Ingeniously, he devised some attractive structured but open-ended tasks which invited his students to pursue questions of the 'What if . . .?' variety. Within a few hours on-line, they had mastered understanding of certain fundamental principles of macro-economics, to an extent which would have been impossible in the old days, when lecturers lectured. In the past, students who set out to explore speculative questions had needed to slog for so long to obtain (particular) results that they had no energy left to see generalizations, and may well have generated sufficient errors in their calculations to obscure the generalizations in any case.

With the use of the software and the database, plenty of examples could be rapidly explored, and analysed comparatively, in richly resourced reflection which led to the desired deep understanding and learning. That learning outcome had not been achieved hitherto, despite the outlay of considerable effort and teaching and learning time.

Example 3.3: New technologies promote reflection – in classics

Changes are currently being introduced in Open University classics courses. In pilot form, students can have access to the full text on CD-ROM of the works they are studying, and to other learning resource materials; they can then be provided with simple software to enable them to carry out searches. The learner is thus freed for analysis rather than being tied down, as in the recent past, to the tedious ingathering of data as mere fodder for analytical thinking.

Recently a student who wished to test out a suspicion about the use of similes involving domestic animals and birds in the writings of Homer, was able to instruct a computer to search the texts. It found all the relevant examples in only a few seconds, rather than her having to devote days to inefficient labour based on incomplete indexes and tedious hand-searching methods. The viability of her initial hypothesis could be quickly checked, and might perhaps have led to the rejection of the enquiry – but in this case it justified further work. She was then not merely freed to engage in, and direct, the analysis which led her to a deeper understanding of Homer's use of simile, she could also do so because the computer could bring together, within a short time scale, all the information acquired and required.

The mere transcription of textual material on to a computerized record, together with the availability of fairly straightforward software which enables textual or similar searches through recorded data to be made, has freed learners of classics to proceed directly into analysis and reflection thereon – without being hampered by the time demanded for searching, or exhausted by the effort devoted to that menial activity. Of course, this situation also has its demanding flipside. For with the humdrum tasks delegated to the new technologies, it only remains for the learner to engage with the demanding development and exercise of higher level cognitive abilities. This in turn calls inexorably for reflection on process – until someone finds a more effective way of developing higher level abilities.

Comment on Examples 3.1–3.3

In these three examples, we saw that the students of mathematics no longer need to spend time learning to differentiate and integrate; for calculators, let alone computers, can do all of that for them. The students of economics can leave routine data-sifting to the computer; they can harness the power of the computer to enable them to grasp concepts which could scarcely be conveyed in traditional teaching, although that understanding is essential for graduates in a world where they must manage the computers which now do what yesterday's graduates used to try to do (tediously) by hand. The students of classics – when enabled to undertake analysis on a scale and with a thoroughness which was inconceivable half a century ago – are challenged by the march of technology to develop fully, and to use profoundly, abilities which in the past were only marginally developed.

Thus learners in all of these discipline areas are nowadays freed to move on to higher educational efforts; and they can do so in learning activities where the speed and coverage of the computer makes it possible for the first time. This in turn encourages concentration on learning about the process of learning, by giving the students and their teachers the opportunity and the time to think about (or rather to reflect on) how best to develop understanding, or to analyse, or to find and solve problems, without a heavy demand on them to carry out tedious and low-level work.

Each of these examples has thus featured two consequences of the advent of the new technologies. First, much of what students used to learn and do is obsolete, because the machine now does it, and does it better than humans; thus students and graduates have to think more deeply, and to operate more consistently at the higher end of the cognitive continuum than ever in the past. The second consequence is the potential to develop abilities purposefully through planned reflection – which was neglected in the past. Because the volume of available data or experiences was massive, the amount of information which could be extracted by laborious methods was slight, and the demands of humdrum tasks left no time for the teaching and learning of higher level abilities. But as my examples show, that option is now entirely possible, and is to be achieved through reflection on the generalities emerging from a wealth of now accessible data which can readily be manipulated by the new technologies.

Example 3.4: The demand for capability – and the implications for reflection

In 1980, a number of prominent British personalities came together to formulate the 'Education for Capability' manifesto (Royal Society of Arts, 1980). I leave that document to speak for itself, and simply reproduce here the criteria which it set out for any education which it felt would develop capability. These criteria were regarded at that time as both radical and controversial, even after making due allowance for the status of the majority of the signatories.

Criteria for Education for Capability

The Committee believe that the following criteria must underpin any programme designed to educate for capability:

1. the demonstrated competence of the learners is increased, particularly through active methods of learning which develop the existing interests, skills and experiences of the learners;

2. the capacity to cope is developed by encouraging learners to find solutions to problems which they have personally identified, in contexts relevant to their own lives;
3. the creative abilities of learners are drawn upon and expanded through doing, making and organizing;
4. learners are encouraged to get on with other people, and to initiate and engage in co-operative activity;
5. learners are involved, according to their maturity, in negotiating with their teachers what it is they need to learn;
6. programmes are accessible to a wide range of learners;
7. methods of assessing and giving recognition to successful performance are appropriate to the activity undertaken;
8. the aims and objectives of the programme are understood and accepted by learners and staff; and
9. there is a coherent programme design with effective execution.

It is only fair to give to these campaigners due credit for a number of consequent initiatives which were taken up by secondary and tertiary education in Britain in the 1980s. Notably these commenced with the widespread promotion of Education for Capability, through the Royal Society of Arts (RSA) recognition scheme. Later this trend continued in universities through the Enterprise in Higher Education initiative, which was in effect launched by the British government, and funded accordingly. More recently, there has been the move to offer vocational qualifications at Levels 4 and 5; these will specify outcomes of further and higher education which should be able to be applied in a workplace, and will attempt to assess them accordingly.

None of these developments originated within further or higher education. The original Education for Capability Committee included relatively few academics, yet powerfully pinpointed what they saw as a fundamental weakness in education which did not develop 'appropriate' abilities. This committee attempted to rectify that omission, on behalf of society and particularly, perhaps, of employers. Their recognition scheme encouraged, approved and commended the purposeful development of capability. In my own case, I found that an RSA Award gave my work (Cowan, 1980b) credibility almost overnight, and made it very much easier for me to launch the next innovations (Cowan, 1984b).

The many achievements in education for capability which were recognized by the RSA Award Scheme showed that the most effective programmes attributed a great deal of their success to the encouragement of structured reflection on learning processes and on the abilities used to meet the criteria. Those who set out to follow such pioneers naturally judged it worthwhile to adopt similar teaching methods, as they attempted to repeat and to better their successes. They tended to be successful in their turn, and so – empirically – the need to arrange for the contribution of reflection was endorsed by what Education for Capability programmes had achieved.

You will notice, however, that the manifesto and the criteria did not explicitly call for reflection on the process of learning itself. That was not to become a distinctive feature of progressive education, other than in the most adventurous innovations, until the current decade.

Example 3.5: A particular need for qualitative understanding – and reflective learning

In the 1970s, coming from different starting points, Brohn (1973) and I (Cowan, 1975, 1977) attempted to demonstrate to those responsible for the education of structural engineers that there were serious weaknesses in their objectives, as well as in the outcomes they were achieving. Separately at first, and later together (Brohn and Cowan, 1977), we devised and used tests which showed that students who were able to 'number crunch' sufficiently well to gain a good honours degree might nevertheless have no grasp whatsoever of the behaviour of the structures for which they were able to carry out these complex calculations.

In my case, I worked with students who (as graduates) would often be required to appreciate the behaviour of the structural members of a bridge or a roof truss. If they were told the loadings which that structure was required to sustain, they could readily (if tediously) calculate the forces in each of the members. Their examination performances confirmed this ability. Yet, if I showed them a photograph or a diagram of a bridge or a roof truss, with a real load or loads in position; and if I asked them merely which members would be in tension (being stretched) and which members would be in compression (being crushed), I usually found that they were incapable of giving me an answer – other than by first carrying out calculations, or by what virtually amounted to guesswork (Cowan, 1981b). They lacked what I had come to call qualitative understanding (Cowan, 1980c).

In Brohn's case, he showed convincingly (Brohn, 1973) that good honours graduates, entering employment with one of the top consultants in the country, could carry out calculations which produced what are called 'bending moment diagrams' – but that, without first carrying out these calculations, they could not anticipate, even approximately, the shape of diagram they were expecting to produce. Thus, if a computer to which they had given incorrect data produced an erroneous diagram for them, they wouldn't notice the error.

We reported our findings to the Institution of Structural Engineers (Brohn and Cowan, 1977) and to some of our colleagues in the teaching profession. Practising engineers confirmed our concern and the grounds for it. They expressed supportive horror at what we described at that time as a widespread lack of qualitative understanding of structural behaviour, among students on courses where quantitative understanding, or at least the ability to carry out routine calculations, was already a proven and valued skill.

The teaching profession, who had at first expressed frank disbelief at our findings, gradually accepted the importance of qualitative understanding; and some have attempted remedial measures within existing curricula. These initiatives have been, on the whole, unsuccessful – in my opinion because they have depended on didactic instruction ('I'll tell you how to do it – or rather how I think *I* do it') which is an ineffective and inappropriate way of developing cognitive abilities, as I will suggest in the next chapter. Few teachers persisted in their efforts to achieve what they resignedly accepted was an impossible objective. Traditional curricula across the country (and in Europe) have not significantly altered. The hidden curriculum of assessment, as revealed in examination papers, has barely changed; and the profession still bewails the lack of qualitative ability on the part of graduates emerging from the system.

Qualitative understanding is clearly a required and valued professional ability in engineering – but it is even now only being recognized and developed in certain innovative curricula. It was my desire to rectify this weakness in my own curriculum, through understanding the ways in which students ineffectively handled qualitative analysis, which led me to engage in research using recorded protocols (Cowan, 1983). I needed to discover what was happening, and what was not happening, when my students attempted problems which called for the exercise of qualitative understanding. I then built on my initial enquiries to develop a style of tutorial question (Cowan, 1982) which literally demanded qualitative understanding, and offered no return for quantitative understanding – in other words, I introduced problems where a solution could not be obtained merely by applying formulae and carrying out routine calculations, but called instead for the application of deep conceptual understanding. (These problems, incidentally, often proved insuperable for conventional lecturers, accustomed to following algorithms rather than thinking.)

Gradually it became clear to me that there was a difference akin to an order of magnitude between the two types of understanding – for quantitative understanding merely required the student to be able to carry out routine calculations in familiar settings while qualitative understanding called for a sound grasp of concepts. My subsequent design of learning and teaching situations to develop qualitative understanding relied heavily on a reflective approach to process, and was measurably effective (Cowan, 1986b). This contrasted starkly with the teaching and learning situations then in common use in further and higher engineering education, which satisfactorily achieved the lower level of quantitative understanding through employing didactic instruction to drill students to assimilate and use standard algorithms, of whose basis they did not necessarily have any understanding, deep or otherwise.

I believe that this example shows the importance to professional performance of deep learning at higher cognitive levels, which cannot be purposefully developed in education without arranging for the learner to reflect on both concepts and processes.

Example 3.6: The viability of reflective learning is demonstrated on a large scale

It was some 25 years ago that the Principal of Alverno College in Milwaukee asked her faculty colleagues to pause and to review their educational activities. She suggested to them that they should reconsider the nature of the higher education which they offered to their students. She questioned the very suitability of that education, in the context of the society from which the students came, to which they would certainly be returning, and within which they would be working and living.

The result of these deliberations was a fundamental change in the nature of the higher education programme which was offered at Alverno College. The details of this radical and innovatory institution have been summarized elsewhere (Heywood, 1989; George, 1992). Suffice it to say here that, instead of dealing in the traditional way with subject matter and content coverage, the faculty concentrated on the development of abilities, in the broadest sense of that phrase. They achieved this by encouraging reflective awareness of process, thoroughly integrated with comprehensive coverage and mastery of content. In addition, instead of continuing with a system in which assessment by teachers alone provided the ultimate judgement on a student's competence and development, the college moved dramatically to a situation in which reflective self-assessment was encouraged and recognized from the outset (Loacker *et al.*, 1986).

Having made that change, this small college in the Mid-West of the United States found itself one of the most described, most visited and most praised institutions of higher education in the English-speaking world. Visitors of high educational status have trekked from all quarters of the globe to Milwaukee, and have thus testified that the world of higher education has judged the Alverno development and found it valuable. That judgement surely endorses *inter alia* the strong emphasis placed on reflection within the Alverno model of higher education.

I take Alverno College as the supreme example of the change which can occur – and in their case did occur – when an educational programme and its methods are appraised and redesigned in accordance with the abilities which represent the current needs of society, rather than the timeworn and outdated priorities of educationists in higher education. For our present purposes, I pinpoint one feature of the Alverno College development and experience which is highly relevant to the question at the head of this chapter. Faced with the challenge from within to create, or re-create, an educational programme suitable for the external society, Alverno came up with something radically different from the status quo. It chose to focus on abilities as heavily as on content mastery – and to develop these abilities through reflective self-assessment and reflective awareness of process.

Other examples

- Recent developments in design education at UK secondary school level have produced a generation of school leavers who are accustomed to reflect on the processes they follow when engaged in creative design. They expect that pattern of teaching and learning activity, which has proved profitable for their learning, to continue when they move into higher education. They are often disappointed.
- In schemes for continuing professional development, the identification of needs and the planning of developmental activity rests with the professionals themselves, and they must increasingly depend on their ability to reflect – analytically

and evaluatively. These schemes presume (often wrongly) that this reflective ability will have been developed before graduation.

- Workplace-based learning, which is nowadays a valued constituent of vocational courses in higher education, depends on purposeful reflection to bring about the generalized learning which is desired.

Non-examples

It is neither desirable nor effective to depend primarily on reflective learning when:

- The learners are being helped to master a standard procedure which they will often have to apply as specified.
- Learners are required to acquire and store, and eventually recall, a vast range of facts.
- The objective is for the learner to develop psychomotor skills, such as ten-finger keyboard skills.

Generalization

We now live in an age in which information is generated at a worrying rate, and in which, at the same time, information becomes obsolete at a terrifying rate. It has been stated that the half-life of an electronic engineer is about two years. In other words, within two years the effectiveness of an electronic engineer has deteriorated by half. Whatever the truth of that assertion, I suspect that few would disagree with the suggestion that information in all discipline areas is being generated at an ever-increasing rate, is becoming obsolete more and more quickly, and is increasingly being handled by telematics rather than by individuals.

Much of the need to devote curriculum time and emphasis to communicating knowledge and developing understanding has now evaporated, because today's knowledge goes rapidly out of date, and computers will supply what we need, when we need it, in any case. Tomorrow's graduates will be more concerned to use understanding than to acquire it. Fortunately, time is now available in any course programme for the development of the abilities which use understanding. New technology now makes possible the development of these abilities which could not be properly exercised and developed previously – because the preliminaries were so demanding, or because there was not time for their development, or both.

Consequently we no longer need to require educated people to grasp long-established and enduring information, and understand it (Cowan, 1984a). Rather, we require the development of the higher level abilities of being able to *apply* information and even machine-held understanding, of being able to *analyse* situations and see potential for development, of being *creative* in suggesting ways in which development therein should occur and can be supported, and of being *evaluative* – both in formatively judging recent activities and in creatively judging proposals for activities yet to be translated into the reality of action. We also increasingly appreciate the importance of the interpersonal skills and understanding of relationships which have always mattered but have not, until recently, figured prominently in most academic curricula.

Unfortunately teachers in further and higher education are regrettably ignorant about the choice and use of pedagogical methods which are suitable for an education which concentrates more and more on higher level cognitive and inter-personal abilities. Consequently the immediate challenge to higher education in particular is to develop purposefully the abilities which society, the professions, and our paymasters value – and which they seek as an outcome of our highly expensive arrangements for education. Unfortunately, there is at present still a regrettable lack of congruence within education between the abilities which matter, and the abilities which are purposefully and deliberately developed.

Some educationists, and especially those concerned with mature and often graduate learners, have devoted considerable effort in recent years to eradicating this anomaly. They have sought pedagogies and practices for teaching and learn-ing situations which will effectively foster the outcomes which society, mature adults and employers increasingly seek – and indeed expect. In the practices which have to date proved successful in this respect, we find that most innovators have committed themselves to giving a key role to reflection.

In a tentative summary, therefore, I suggest that:

- There are apparent mismatches between the abilities and outcomes pursued in traditional further and higher education, and those needed in professional life or felt desirable in the interests of society – or both.
- Social and professional pressures have been brought to bear in recent years, to demand changes to make all education more valid and appropriate – and they continue to be a powerful influence in the reshaping of education.
- Institutions which manage to change their curricula to take note of economic or social needs are valued by society and students alike.
- The new technologies render the acquisition of basic knowledge, and the hand-ling of that knowledge, less and less important; and they place more weight on the higher level cognitive and interpersonal abilities, which in turn call for rad-ically different pedagogies – if teaching and learning are to be effective.
- To date, such pedagogies have given reflection a central place in their method-ologies.
- The results obtained by those educators who stimulate reflection on the process of learning itself (which is nowadays called metacognition) justify a sea change in our approach to the design of much of what is done in education, at least for adults.
- Reflection offers real hope of meeting tomorrow's needs and demands in edu-cation.

Before you test this, some second thoughts from me

1. Many would argue that we cannot teach communication skills without getting students to communicate. Similarly, it can be held that we cannot develop

creativity unless the students are concurrently engaged in creative activity within their studies; and that we cannot develop analytical powers unless the students are engaged in being analytical, with meaningful subject matter and valid analytical tasks. An observer visiting Alverno, for example, could point immediately to the impressive way analytical ability is developed and assessed within the context of the subjects which are being studied. So is it not artificial, and hence bad pedagogical practice, to attempt to separate out the abilities, and to concentrate separate attention on the reflection or other distinct activity which seeks to develop them?

2. One could further argue that the educational system has always sought – and with considerable success – to develop the abilities which have mattered to society of the time and for the professions; and that it has done so – until now – without separately concentrating on reflection. Thus it follows that no fundamental change in the existing system should be necessary to provide what is now apparently needed, although like all processes, the status quo may well offer scope for improvement and refinement. If the abilities now demanded are emphasized differently, surely that does not in itself justify a call for different teaching methods?

3. The Education for Capability manifesto only specifies outcomes; similarly many educational developments nowadays, such as the vocational ones, concentrate on outcomes and give little guidance on process. However desirable these developments may be, can we give credence to initiatives which (perhaps naively) set out to achieve radically changed outcomes without giving thought or attention to the means of so doing, and the necessary changes in learning and teaching methods?

4. Is there a useful parallel here with the enduring example of education in arts and performance skills, or in an artistic discipline such as architecture? What occurs there is and always has been heavily dependent on intuitions and aspirations which are arguably not in the artist's voluntary control, and may not be of a kind that can ever be given explicit verbal utterance. But in all such artistic processes, including those which occur in educational situations, there are critical moments of feedback, of taking stock, of applying general principles (and of deliberately and consciously going against some accepted principles or criteria) – all of which involve reflective thought and judgement. This is what the best artists and their pupils have always done in relation to their own work. It is how reflective learning occurs and is promoted in these disciplines; for making art is impossible without analytical and evaluative reflection.

This well-established example of professional development and effective education should perhaps act as our model – and perhaps also as a source of shame to the professions and institutions whose education is more pedestrian. Does it prompt us, for example, to accept that important mental processes cannot always be articulated or even internalized, although they can still be judged by their outcomes?

Dear John

You've suggested that the world is changing, and that the world of education needs to change in turn. So I'm beginning to be persuaded that this reflection thing could be something I should try out in my own courses and teaching. But I need help with that, because I can't just imitate your examples. You and I teach different subjects, in different situations. I need some guiding principles or models to follow, or a way to transform some of your examples into my situation.

At the moment, to be frank, it all sounds rather like a good idea which some innovators like you have taken up with enthusiasm, and from which they have managed to produce some interesting results. But that doesn't mean that it's a sound idea; the positive outcomes could be the result of the well-known phenomenon of novelty bringing improved performance – for a short time.

Can you show me a pedagogical rationale, or an underlying methodology which I can understand and follow?

4

Is There a Methodology You Can and Should Follow?

Introduction

I could give you a glib answer to that question immediately. While Karl Popper would, I suppose, advise us that a theory in this area cannot be proven, Skemp (1979) maintains stoutly that there is nothing as practical as theory. He argues that using theories has three advantages. They tell us what is going on beyond those things which are immediately observable; they reduce 'noise', and allow us to concentrate on what is relevant for the task in hand; and, by having a considerable degree of independence from the examples and classes of examples from which they were constructed, they enable us to make new paths outwards from our thinking.

Let's test out and try to understand Skemp's suggestion (1979: 182) that 'a theory is not itself a model for a particular task, but something much more general: namely a schema within which can be conceptualized all the possible states within a particular universe of discourse, and relations between these states'. But before doing that, please bear with me as I try to distinguish between a theory and a model.

My dictionary suggests to me that, in this type of situation, a model is a representation or a simplified description of a system. I suspect this chapter will mainly be about such models – ways of describing what we are doing, or can do. In contrast, a theory is a supposition or system of ideas based on general principles, providing an explanation of something. I am afraid I have not really encountered anything sufficiently well-founded educationally to explain teaching and learning which is centred on reflection – and certainly nothing which proceeds from a basis of proven principles or with sufficient authority to explain, rather than describe, what happens. So I will try to eschew the use of the word 'theory' from now on, in this chapter, and will describe the ideas I present as models.

I'll begin from an example of a widely used model which purports to explain and represent how reflection fits into the process of learning. Next I will summarize, in a necessarily brief reference, a model of reflection – or rather of two forms of reflection. Then I'll offer you a composite model which attempts to represent what may happen in the type of learning and teaching situation we may arrange to facilitate reflective learning.

After a few examples, I will attempt generalizations to help you with your reflection – and then, since this will have been a chapter with a fair amount of input from me, I will close with rather more than usual in the way of critical second thoughts, on which I hope you will find it productive to ponder.

Model 4.1: The Kolb cycle (Figure 4.1)

I ask you first to revisit Example 2.2 (the Interdisciplinary Studies class) in some detail with me, concentrating on what will be a modestly abstract description of the process which the students were following, albeit covertly and in response to my facilitative prompting. The words which I will highlight in italics in the next paragraph or two will refer to concepts which I have taken from a generalized model of how learning from experience happens. This model is usually attributed to Kolb (1984), although it originated from Lewin (1951). The words, which I also use in the diagram below, are my own, and not Kolb's; it seems that those who quote this diagram often choose to paraphrase in their own terminology.

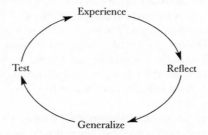

Figure 4.1   The Kolb cycle (using words paraphrased by Cowan)

After they had been introduced to the sequence of activities in my workshop, the first year students in Example 2.2 engaged in active learning, during which they began by drawing on three types of experience. There were the individual experiences which they had all had, in their fairly recent student past, in tackling questions or exercises of the type assembled on the worksheet before them. There was the very recent experience, for each student, of tackling one of these very questions on that particular worksheet. And there were the vicarious or second-hand experiences of their fellow students, reported to fellow members of the working group which had been assembled for this activity. Each student, then, had access to an assortment of *experiences*.

The students were now required by the task structure to *reflect*, and to do so in two subtly different ways, the second being more general and focused than the first. They were first asked to identify how they had tackled a particular question or exercise – which usually led them to a description of that process in what was still fairly particular and rather incomplete terms. This description became refined and generalized somewhat, as pairs of students compared and contrasted their methods. And so they moved, fairly gently and unobtrusively, into the second type of reflection, which proved the bridge from their particular experiences to a generalization. For they tried to stand back from their own experiences, and to *generalize* what, now as a group, they had been doing.

The production of an outline of the method took them to a point at which they could be ready to *test* out their generalization, by using it to solve other examples or problems taken from the same worksheet – these being problems which no one in their group had yet attempted. When they carried out this testing, they would sometimes find that the fresh example contained a twist for which they had not catered in their first survey of experiences. Or they might discover that the way in which their method outline was worded, even if only regarded as advice to themselves, could be phrased in a more appropriate and usefully general form. And so, when they came to *reflect* again after each new *experience*, they could sometimes see that there might well need to be a change in the way they had chosen to *generalize* the overall method or approach to this family of problems – to make it a more effective basis for future problem-solving. In addition, there were the few occasions when tutors had made an input to the process of generalization, which students were then asked to test out against their next experiences.

Thus these students, for at least the one and a half cycles I have described, were exemplifying the description of how experiential learning can happen, according to the model which is known as the Kolb cycle (Figure 4.1). They were being taken purposefully round it by following structured activities devised by their facilitative teacher. In this structure there was a strong concentration on reflection as the bridge from experiences to potentially useful generalization; and there was also an emphasis, not always evident in other attempts to facilitate experiential learning, on the need to test out the generalization purposefully. The students' successes in subsequent problem-solving confirmed the usefulness of this model to them. I suggest that the important existence of the tutor's facilitative inputs indicates a significant omission from this diagram.

In the Kolb diagram, the most important parts are probably the lines between the words, which carry no explanation. Much of the task of the facilitative teacher is to encourage movement around the cycle and hence along these lines. Teachers can bring this about by asking the questions which take the students from experience to reflection; or by introducing the task which moves them out of reflection into generalizing. At the same time, however, there are naturally-occurring events which prompt movement, or lead to flashes of insight or inspiration on the part of the learners. Mismatches between model or generalization and experience are one such stimulus. The students in this example often found that a draft of a general method, which had looked feasible for one or two examples, did not work for the next one, and so had to be refined – and improved. Similarly one problem on the sheet might contain an apparently new feature, which called for reflection to determine how it should be treated.

Model 4.2: The ideas of Schön – and beyond?

An educationist called Schön has written and published a number of popular texts (1983, 1987, 1991) in which he has concentrated on the concept of 'the reflective practitioner'. Schön identifies the reflective practitioner as someone who engages in reflection related to action – or to experiences, in the vocabulary I have been using so far. He writes sometimes of reflection-in-action, and at other times of reflection-on-action. In the examples we have examined, it was of course the students themselves who were being encouraged to become reflective practitioners – quite appropriately, I suggest, in the education of adults.

If we make distinctions, separation can help us to appreciate important subtleties in the items we so separate. I suggest here that the three occasions for reflection which we encountered in Example 2.1 can usefully be distinguished by categorizing them under three headings which make meaningful, and helpful, distinctions for me. Two of these are derived from Schön.

The types of reflection which Schön describes can be found within the experiences of the OU students working on study skills at Dumfries (Example 2.1). In the first half-evening, when they were dealing with a particular skill, the students practised *reflection-on-action*. They cast their minds back and reflected on recent learning experiences, and on what they had done in these situations. They generalized, both about the nature of the difficulties they had encountered and about the style of approach which they had pursued in attempting to deal with the problems. In both cases they were engaging in reflection with hindsight, on recently completed and relatively self-contained experiences. Reflection-on-action mainly looks back on the action contained in past experiences; it attempts to analyse and summarize that past experience, and thereby to extract generalizations which will be of future use.

When the students encountered a learning difficulty in the course of their subsequent studies, they immediately tried to classify it, and to relate it to the advice sheet which the group as a whole had assembled. They went on to respond to, or to modify, the group's advice to its members. At this point they were engaging in *reflection-in-action*, 'stimulated by triggers, patterns and confirmations within the frame of action itself' (Hirschhorn, 1991: 125). In other words, their classification of the new difficulty and their identification for immediate use of the corresponding advice they had generated about that type of difficulty, was leading them immediately on from this reflection to test out and perhaps modify the advice they had helped to set out in the guidance sheet. Reflection-in-action looks backward to immediately past experiences, and forward to experiences which are imminent. It entails as much anticipative thought and analysis as retrospective review. It is a reflection which should, for example, lead to improved or at least carefully premeditated performance.

In the Dumfries pilot, there was also a third type of reflection, which is not specifically titled by Schön. This was what I shall choose to call *reflection-for-action*, that title having been suggested to me by McAleese (1996) when I showed him the diagram we are to meet in the next section (Figure 4.2). In the beginning, the students reflected on difficulties which they had encountered in their studies, and tried to extract examples of that, and to make some classification of these examples. At that time they were – in effect – defining their aspirations for the workshop activity which lay ahead. They were reflecting on types of problem which they hoped to be able to resolve more effectively in the future than in the past. I suggest that this reflection, being anticipatory, is aptly titled reflection-for-action. It is a reflection which establishes priorities for subsequent learning by identifying the needs, aspirations and objectives which will subsequently be kept prominently in the learner's mind.

Schön has written at length and in depth on the concept of the reflective practitioner. It would be impertinent of me to attempt a summary, probably unhelpful for you to encounter his full thesis at this stage, and intrusive to digress in that way in the present text. Please forgive me if that omission irritates or frustrates; Schön is best read in the original, and you have the references. However I feel it vital to point out at this stage that the use of the same word by Kolb and Schön does not imply that they seek to convey similar meaning. Kolbian reflection is a component in a sequence, the bridge to be crossed between particular experience and consequent generalization, an activity carried out with that one, almost closed-ended, purpose in mind. Schönian reflection, in contrast, whichever variant we consider, is an open-ended activity detached to some extent, however briefly, from the action, with outcomes which are not predetermined in nature but are determined within the process, and whose occurrence is not absolutely necessary in order for the action to proceed.

Model 4.3: The Cowan diagram (Figure 4.2)

Some educationists, in the literature or in conference discussions or elsewhere, have suggested that the endless circling of the Kolb cycle, from a beginning which it is difficult to identify, is either depressing or misleading – or both. Some have suggested pulling the coils of the diagram upwards, so that it forms a spiral, reaching ever upwards and onwards. For my own contribution to this debate, I have drawn a diagram rather like an overstretched spring, in my Figure 4.2. This, I submit, is entirely different in principle from a distorted Kolb cycle, since it uses reflection as Schön does and thus highlights the differences between Kolbian and Schönian reflection – of which more shortly.

I will illustrate this model, and that standpoint, by reference to Example 2.3 (Interdisciplinary Studies) – and, afterwards, to Example 2.4 (the Aalborg course).

When the students on the IDS course in Example 2.3 arrived to take part in the programme for a particular week, they all brought with them significant prior experience. Part of this came from their relatively common experience as first year students in my department; but a significant part of it came from a wide assortment of previous learning situations. The activity with which a particular Tuesday afternoon was concerned, while it essentially built on prior experience and depended upon it, therefore began with or from an anticipatory reflection-for-action. This generated a definition of the diverse needs and goals which were relevant to individual students, in relation to the general title declared for the activity which lay ahead.

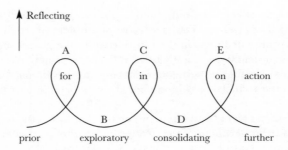

Figure 4.2   The Cowan diagram

Having paused relatively briefly for this reflection-for-action (loop A in Figure 4.2), the students were encouraged to surge forward into an exploratory activity which had been thoughtfully planned for them. In the first burst of that activity (arc B in Figure 4.2), the students unearthed what they already carried in their 'intellectual luggage' which might prove useful to them. They also discovered what they could helpfully borrow, or copy, from that which their fellow students were carrying. They were even invited in part of the activity to explore, and to test for feasibility, some possibly useful ideas which were made available to them by their teachers, and which might not have arisen from within the collective experience of that particular group.

The students 'froze' their thinking on the Tuesday afternoon (loop C in Figure 4.2) with an intermediate reflection-in-action. In this they identified in some detail the progress they had made, the point they had reached in their learning and in how they were thinking – while at the same time expressing in similar detail the difficulties or gaps which now thwarted their further development, and with which they required facilitative assistance. This review at the end of the Tuesday afternoon, which quickly looked back on the work of the previous 90 minutes or so and then equally swiftly looked forward to the challenges for the next morning, was clearly reflection-in-action, because the three-hour workshop was only two-thirds complete.

And so, in due course, the students moved on to the concentrated activity of the Wednesday morning (arc D in Figure 4.2). There they worked on a consolidating input offered by their teachers. They did everything possible to make good the deficiencies which they had perceived in their learning or development, and to build upon their reflective analysis of their progress to date.

They completed our Wednesday morning activity without a 'final' reflection. That was not to take place until the Wednesday evening, by which time the students had had the experience of returning to take part in their more normal student activities. Following that modest opportunity to test out the new development in practice, they were better able to compile their reflective learning journals (loop E in Figure 4.2). You will recall that this reflection was centred on what each had learned about learning or thought about thinking, which should make them more effective in the week ahead than they had been in the week which lay behind. This was therefore a stocktaking activity, and essentially a reflection-on-action. For this reflection identified and defined the useful learning and development which had taken place in actions completed – learning which was now ready to be carried outwards, and put into service, in everyday studying.

There was always the possibility, of course, that the last loop might swiftly become reflection-for-action, if significant new needs were identified or urgent aspirations emerged. If so, the learners moved into another sequence, in which all of the activities I have described here became the prior experience feeding into that next learning sequence.

Comments

We have traced out, in the context of one example, the components of my model (Figure 4.2) wherein the emphasis is on reflections and experiential actions of particular types. You may have noted that, in my zeal to convey the importance of three types of reflection, which call for three types of activity by the learner and hence for three forms of facilitation by the teacher, I seem to have lost by the wayside the other three elements in the Kolb diagram, and the subtle transitions between them.

All of this, I assume, is still included, even if not explicitly described. Examine, for instance, one of those sections between reflective loops, and consider what I have already described to be happening there. Refer, for example, to the IDS programme described in Example 2.3. In the exploratory activity marked by arc B, the groups followed much the same outline of activity as was offered to the Dumfries students, in Example 2.1. They began from familiar examples of their own *experience*, *reflected* quickly on their general features, and attempted to classify them in a *generalization* – and then did the same for methods of response which had, or had not, proved effective for one member at least of the group on one occasion in the past. These are, in effect, two cycles around the Kolb diagram, perhaps adequately represented by inserting coils in the line between the first two major reflective loops in Figure 4.2, as in Figure 4.2.2.

For the reflection in the midst of the workshop action at C, the students stood back slightly from the action, to take just a little time to reflect on what they were doing, how they were tackling it, and – to some extent – what progress they were making and what remained unresolved on their agenda. This was reflection in the

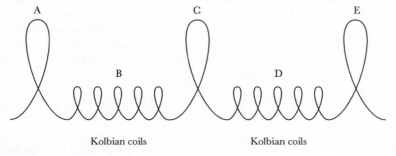

Kolbian coils   Kolbian coils

Figure 4.2.2   Modified Cowan diagram

few minutes which were almost stolen from the action; such reflection can be immensely valuable, because of that very proximity to action. Sometimes, of course, it can be inappropriate, as in the case of a pilot landing a light aircraft in a gale – which is hardly the most suitable occasion for reflection-in-action on how or what he or she learns best from that type of experience (Brown, 1996).

Now consider the second section between loops – at D. For here something rather different was occurring. The facilitators had provided a generalized input, which was intended to be of use to the learners. It was offered as something which the learners should test out – and that testing was the focus for this period of activity. Thus this section of the model covered input, planning to test and the experience of testing – after which the students were left to reflect on what the proffered suggestion had offered them. Fortunately they were soon in a position to move into the review activity of reflection-on-(total)-action of the three-hour workshop, unless they had major unresolved needs to figure as reflection-for-(the next needed)-action. This sequence of events can also be represented in a modification to the basic diagram, by adding another coil of Kolbian activity between Schönian reflections.

Hence I feel that a better diagram would be that of Figure 4.2.2, except for the fact that it would need too many words or letters to explain its subtleties, and would become so complex as to convey no message. I therefore prefer to think in terms of the basic Cowan diagram for the overall outline, and then to expand parts of it, as we have just done in words, when the detail of parts of a programme are being considered – or planned.

Back to the basic Cowan diagram

Now let us relate this model to the Aalborg example (Example 2.4), which appears to me to be an elegant illustration, on a macro scale, of the pedagogy of the Cowan model. Only the formalization at the initial stage of the reflection-for-action stage is absent.

The Aalborg programme begins from the students' prior experience, which accrues, in many cases, from school and from the year after school. It opens, in the P0 project, with the first exploratory surge (B) of the diagram. At the end of that introductory experience, there is ample opportunity for intermediate reflection-in-action (C), facilitated both by students from the previous year, and by supervisors. Then, after this intermediate loop of reflection, the learners surge into the P1 experience (D), after which there is a closing reflection-on-action (E) – and also a reflection-for-action (A), which precedes the move into the P2 project, and the next journey through the diagram.

Other examples

- The stimulus/response model which originated from Skinner and the behaviourists (Leith, 1969) was the theoretical model which underpinned many of the

early developments in programmed learning in the 1960s.
- A teacher's simple statement of belief in 'telling them what to do, getting them to do that, and then reminding them what they have done' is a theoretical framework which underlies many programmes of instruction (however successful) which have the development of cognitive abilities in mind.
- Boud and Walker (1993) have a model of the reflection processes in learning from experience in which they emphasize three concepts which are important to them: a personal foundation of experience, intent, and preparation.

A non-example

- The detailed description in Example 2.3, while reasoned and explained, is in itself neither a (generalized) theory nor a model.

My generalizations towards a theoretical framework

A theory can be regarded as a network of concepts, which are linked together in a coherent framework which allows for testing against evidence and the prediction or planning of action. I hope you may find it useful to accumulate some concepts for your own network and theory of reflective learning, from your judgement of the particular example of my Cowan diagram.

I submit that my diagram (Figure 4.2) is useful, for a start, because it highlights the existence of three different purposes for reflection. It also distinguishes between analytical and evaluative reflection. Analytical reflection concentrates on finding the answers to such questions as 'How do I do it?' or 'How should I do it?' The intermediate reflection-in-action (C), while it undoubtedly also includes a slight evaluative element, is predominantly analytical; for it entails cataloguing and summarizing and specifying that which has been learned, and identifying the gaps and inconsistencies therein which require further developmental attention. In contrast, the evaluative type of reflection (E) mainly addresses the question 'How well can I do it?' or 'Should I do it better?' This is a stocktaking which judges the development which has already taken place or is needed. While summarizing development analytically, it more importantly identifies whether or not the learning is adequate to enable the learner to go off into other activities, including those in which the new learning will be used; or alternatively, whether the learner needs to go into a further set of developmental experiences, in order to make the desired progress. Of course, there is also at this point the possibility of a rather different type of analytical reflection, which poses the further question 'What is it that I need to be able to do?' This can occur at E or at A and is, I submit, an analytical specification of need, with some evaluative overtones.

My diagram links together the concepts advanced by Schön and the relationships postulated by Kolb. It is compatible with the writings of Schön (Model 4.2), and has been duly derived from Kolb (Model 4.1). Hence it appears to provide a fairly sound and practical model to explain, or at least to predict, how experiential learning can happen, and is a model which is developing with practice and is influenced by it, as well as influencing it in turn.

Testing my own generalization

Do I use the model – and does it work? Unless these two questions can be answered satisfactorily, the generalization I have attempted to encapsulate is immediately suspect.

For three years, Derek Fordyce and I designed virtually all our IDS activities with this model in our minds, as guidance rather than as a prescription. We planned our activities with different purposes and hence in different forms, according to which of the three reflections we hoped to facilitate. In the first loop, we felt that we had to provide an effective activity which would help students to define needs and aspirations more specifically than before, as their reflection-for-action. The second had to be a brisk part-activity to round off the work of the Tuesday afternoon, when we and they needed a snapshot of the current state of their learning. So Derek and I had to conceive an activity for that loop which encouraged and enabled students to stand apart from or above the action in which they had already been immersed for 90 minutes or so, and to summarize what they were doing, how they were doing that, how successful and unsuccessful it was being, and whether they had made progress with their needs or now wished to redefine them with more clarity – all as reflection-in-action. The final reflection-on-action had to facilitate a different type of activity again, in which the students would be helped either to summarize succinctly what they were taking from the activity and would hope to put to later use, or what remained unresolved, which then became a potential need leading into reflection-for-further-action.

In the surges of activity between loops, which were the main part of our programme, we planned for testing, generalizing and new experiences to provoke reflection on process, with an awareness of the need for that coverage of the entire Kolb cycle which is not, I admit, explicitly conveyed in my diagram. I would excuse myself by suggesting that no single diagram can represent every facet of what we do. Since the models are descriptive and not prescriptive, it is perhaps useful to see them as separate screens to lay over the process – while we see what we can learn from it – rather than prescriptions to be followed exactly. Postle (1993), for instance, stresses the affective dimension, which I hope you will see from my examples is important for me, but which (again) I have not managed to make explicit in this model of mine.

We judged our effectiveness against the intentions which we derived from this model, which I had developed and continued to refine through our developmental work together. So it was certainly something that we used constantly, for it was the shorthand of our communication with each other – as it was later when Judith George and I designed our rather different workshop activities, in different circumstances and for different target groups.

Did it – the model – work, though, as a simple and helpful description of our process? We did not present it overtly to our students; but we described it to them if they enquired about the unusual sequence of workshop activities which they were going through. We found that, in the learning journals, students would relate their thinking to particular points on the 'loopy diagram', as they called it. A learning journal might contain the statement, for example, that 'What I've just written in some ways makes up for the fact that our group didn't manage to get over the top in the middle loop, on Tuesday afternoon'. And the evaluation of IDS, which I conducted systematically by examining the impact of the programme on the performance of our students in subjects which Derek and I were not their teachers (Cowan, 1986a), showed that the programme had had an impact on their learning – although I admit that this does not confirm the model as the cause of that. Still, there is a close correlation between my use of the model in planning and presentation, and our effect through IDS on the development of their interdisciplinary abilities.

Generalizations

For the reasons I have set out, I have some confidence in asserting that:

- Kolb's cycle is generally accepted and used to describe the constructive relationships between experiencing, reflecting, generalizing, and planning to test out generalizations.
- Schön has established the fairly well-accepted concepts of reflection-in-action and reflection-on-action as significant contributions to learning and development.
- There appears a sound case to argue a place, in addition, for reflection-for-action.
- Kolb and Schön rely on reflection for rather different purposes – Kolb as a bridge to generalization, and Schön as a detached review with unspecified goals.
- Kolb's model does not incorporate reflection which is primarily evaluative, rather than analytical.
- The present models which figure reflection in higher education, while providing a framework for curriculum development and evaluation, leave important questions still unanswered, as I will suggest in the next chapter. They are nevertheless valuable because they highlight such issues, in addition to introducing pedagogic structure to the planning of courses and of course activities.

Before you test this, some second thoughts from me

1. None of the thinking I have summarized in this chapter says anything to us directly about the role of the teacher as facilitator. Yet this is obviously of paramount importance, if reflective learning is to occur other than by chance or good fortune.
2. None of the models describe or offer guidance about the times when it will be useful for teachers to provide inputs which draw on the accumulated knowledge of the discipline.

3. In an early version of the Cowan diagram, I included a mirror image above the diagram which I have presented here, rather as if two series of loops and arcs had been sketched on two faces of a Toblerone packet, which had then been flattened out. The loops touched when tutor and learner were in close contact, and ran away from each other – in the three dimensions of the Toblerone packet especially – when the learner was active and the tutor was 'in reserve', or merely available. It is perhaps unfortunate that this version was dropped by me because some people found it an unwelcome complication. For it tried to describe a missing and important element, which is the varying relationship between tutor and student in this process of facilitated learning or development.

4. We must beware of the assumption of linear progress in all of the models I have described. In Chapter 2 alone, each of the examples I have given reminds me that I have found that learners may take one particular experience, reflect on it and hence assemble a fragment of generalization. They may then return to another particular experience, reflecting and again partially generalizing. And so they can go on, oscillating between the two perhaps four or five times, before eventually being ready (or being prompted) to move into the next stage, that of testing or what Kolb calls active experimentation (Figure 4.3). It takes repeated oscillations of that type before they prepare to test out the now fairly complete and considered generalization on new examples and in new experiences. There would appear to be a tendency for some progress within the Kolb cycle to be an erratically incomplete and repetitive use of only part of the diagram, as I have symbolized in Figure 4.3.

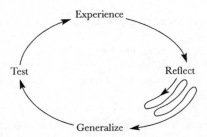

Figure 4.3   Fragmentary progress round the Kolb cycle

5. Evaluative reflection is often an extremely powerful component of development, especially insofar as it identifies needs, aspirations and objectives. But can evaluative reflection of the type I encapsulated in reflection-for-action (as well as in part of reflection-in-action) lead to a generalization (or a theory or an abstraction), in the way that Kolb describes?

6. Each interaction between student and student, and between student and teacher, is a vital element in the process of reflective learning. There are, however, important pedagogical differences between situations which involve synchronous and asynchronous contact between tutor and learner. The pause which attracts no attention between question and formulation of response, and between response and further question from the learner, can entirely change the

nature of interaction and hence of active learning. This has been interestingly of note in the use of fax machines in the Open University in Scotland for what have been called 'fax tutorials' (Rosier, 1998) – in which the potential of asynchronous communication was deliberately harnessed.

7. There may well be significant differences between the person-to-person interactions which facilitate reflection, and interaction with oneself, in private reflection. Thinking processes in each case must presumably interact with linguistic processes, for both to develop and for learning to occur. Is there not a difference between reflection which takes place in spoken or in written words? If so, then we as teachers must decide which of these it is best to encourage in terms of their potential for our students, in given situations where we set out to structure reflection with a chosen purpose.

8. This chapter has not addressed theoretical understanding of the processes we are trying to harness, and has merely concentrated on empirically justified models chosen to describe or advocate effective practice. How, then, shall we progress to a sound theoretical basis for the use of reflection in the development of learners?

Dear John

So far you've given me a reasonable overall description of what you are choosing to call reflection. You've also, in the passing, provided a set of examples of the use of reflection in developing valuable abilities in higher education.

However, if I'm going to give it a try — and I haven't committed myself to that yet — I would want to know more about the detail of what I would need to do, as a university teacher, in this new set-up.

You see, almost all of my teaching experience has been in lecturing, or with running seminars and small group activities which depend on me as the tutor. I just cannot imagine how I would even begin, in the type of settings you describe. How would I persuade my students to engage in reflection, as you define it? Come to think of it, I don't know how I would explain to them what they should do. What can I do to help my students to reflect effectively?

5

What Can You Do to Encourage Students to Reflect?

An apology

I'm afraid I cannot resist temptation. The 'letter' which you have just read tempts me, irresistibly, to divert myself from going straight into examples which describe learners being prompted to reflect, and teachers calling for that reflection. My reason for this prevarication is that I worry lest my questioner is picturing teaching rather differently from the way I do. That's why, before I begin to answer the question at the head of this chapter, I want to table for you – and for me – my interpretation of what the concept of 'teaching' means.

What is 'teaching'?

I take 'teaching' to be:

> the purposeful creation of situations from which motivated learners should not be able to escape without learning or developing.

I put considerable stress in that definition on the word 'purposeful'. It is the existence of a purpose, and the pursuit of it, which for me distinguish education as a process from other situations in which learning occurs. Education, for me, is a process which involves and uses teachers, and hence is distinct from the natural (and valuable) learning or development which will often happen incidentally or accidentally, yet is totally tutorless and learner-directed.

I link learning and development in my definition, because I believe that the highest cognitive learning is about the *development* of cognitive skills rather than the incidental exercise of them in mastering particular content within individual subject contexts.

You'll notice that, according to my definition, I see (and hope for) the real possibility of an active, and even a proactive, role for the facilitative teacher. I subscribe wholeheartedly to the philosophy advanced by Carl Rogers (1951, 1961, 1969, 1983), who likens the facilitative teacher to the therapeutic counsellor. For the questions and comments of the therapeutic counsellor are carefully chosen and are purposefully intended to be constructive, although the counsellor may not always know in which direction they will lead. The same could and should be said of the facilitative teacher in open learning.

Where is all this leading me – and you? For my part, I hope I have established that facilitation can be described as teaching, and that teaching need not involve instruction.

I further suggest, as a basis for the grouping of my examples in this chapter, that there are facilitative teaching and learning situations in which the influence of the teacher in achieving purpose is restricted to the provision of the initial structures and tasks; and that there are also those wherein the engagement of the teacher continues throughout the learner's pursuit of tasks or activities, and may lead to some almost disruptive interventions.

I offer, first, some examples of teaching which facilitates by providing structure in the learning situation. I leave the second type of proactive facilitation till later, since it is provocatively nearer to the authoritarian model of teaching which I would call instructing, and with which we are both undoubtedly familiar.

Example 5.1: Creating a constructive occasion for reflection-for-action

Shortly after they had entered Heriot-Watt University, I arranged that my first year students would attend an introductory meeting where I stressed the importance of communication skills for engineers. At the end, I asked them to declare their learning needs under this heading. In (perhaps) a mildly cynical and certainly self-satisfied manner, most of them indicated politely that they had heard all of this before. They had experienced and profited from an abundance of education and training in communication skills in their school lives. They thus felt adequately prepared for what would presumably be fairly straightforward demands in this first year of their university studies. In other words, while not unwilling to declare outstanding needs, they produced sparse, and sometimes totally blank, lists when they were asked to do so.

Once they had assembled in class for the first time, I invited them to choose a partner with whom they would work for the afternoon. Having done that, they were surprised when I immediately split each pair, and arranged that they were taken away in different directions by tutors who assembled groups of about ten students, in rooms which contained a piece of strange apparatus. The tutor reminded them briefly that one of their tasks in laboratory and experimental project work is to describe apparatus adequately. The tutor next asked them to describe on paper the particular piece of apparatus before them, in the most effective manner possible, and for the benefit of their partners. The tutor indicated willingness to answer any questions about the apparatus, its use and mechanisms – and did so when asked. The students, split from their partners, were encouraged to consult with any of the others in the room, while they each prepared their separate descriptions.

When the descriptions were complete, a postman or postwoman collected them and carried them to another room, containing the second half of each of the split pairs; she or he returned with the descriptions which had been prepared in that room by these partners, who had been faced by a totally different piece of equipment. In both rooms, the students were now invited to comment constructively on the descriptions prepared by their partners.

It was at this point that most of the students discovered that they had made a truly unfortunate choice of partner. For they had opted for someone who was apparently incapable of producing a description which could be comprehended, because it failed to convey all the information which they, the readers, felt that they needed. Happily their tutor encouraged them to annotate the description they had received, indicating where they found it lacking, what additional information they wished, and also those parts of it which they found confusing or were unable to comprehend. Shortly the postperson went into action a second time, carrying the descriptions and requests for clarification and amplification back to their originators.

Most of the students now discovered, a second time and with even more intensity, that they had made a foolish choice of partner. For the person who had received their clear and explicit description had asked all sorts of silly questions about it, had failed to understand points which it undoubtedly conveyed with devastating clarity, and generally had displayed an inability to think, as well as to understand. However the authors were given an opportunity to revise their descriptions, so that – this time, and bearing in mind the undoubted limitations of their partners – the important information about the piece of apparatus in their room would be effectively, if painstakingly, conveyed. Once again, they could consult with others in the same room, seeking advice, inspiration and (often) sympathy.

A second time the descriptions were carried back and forth, to partners. The partners now worked individually and were prohibited from consulting the other students in the room, or their paperwork. They were immediately asked and required to answer ten fair questions about the piece of apparatus in the other room, which was described to them on the piece of paperwork which they were now studying. A fair question was taken to be one which asked for a rough estimate of the size of the piece of apparatus, or the location of the on/off switch, or an indication of the function of the wheels, levers and switches by which the apparatus would be operated. An unfair question would be one which asked about colour (unless that was particularly significant) or the name of the maker. The questions were chosen so that none of the students who had described the apparatus could reasonably quibble with the question list, since it contained only requests for information which should have been provided in their description. Therefore their partner, having been in communication with them, should have been able to answer correctly, from their descriptions. Or should, at least, have been able to score nine out of ten in the total test.

The sheets were quickly self-marked, according to answers provided by the tutors. Few partners scored more than half marks. It was at this stage announced that the mark scored by the recipient for a description would be the mark awarded to the writer or artist of the description. Descriptions and marks were returned to the writers – and the pairs were reunited. But perhaps reunited is not an apt description, for a number of embryo friendships had, by this time, been rather bruised by the experience. Indeed, on the first occasion I ran this activity, one of my colleagues urgently advocated the need to lay on coffee and chocolate biscuits, to restore the blood sugar level, and the equilibrium, of some of the more agitated students.

Most of the students had by then concluded without intervention from the tutors that they had quite a lot to learn about the simple task of describing a piece of apparatus, and even about comprehending a description of a piece of apparatus. From the unprompted reflections which rather frenetically began when the process went so badly wrong, there had emerged a particular type of generalization – namely a generalization which specified learning needs, and was a consequence of what I have chosen to call reflection-for-action (Model 4.2). The aim of the activity had been achieved; the students already knew what they could not do effectively, and had almost identified the objectives they now wanted help with – help they had rejected shortly before this event. All concerned retired to ponder over their continuing reflections on this experience.

In this example, the students had an experience which led them to reflect on their competence, and to generalize their learning needs accordingly. That sequence appears to be almost self-contained. It tempts me to enquire if sometimes (and possibly in more examples than this one) it is unnecessary to go round the Kolb cycle more than once, or even to go round it completely, before some learning outcomes are achieved. Yet my experiences elsewhere suggest the value of repeated experiences and cycling.

It was the structure of this activity, and not any subsequent actions by any tutor, which led students to rethink their self-judgement about their ability to undertake the simple task of describing apparatus. And so, with their needs perceived, they were prepared to commence their learning journeys to resolve these needs.

Example 5.2: Structured dialogue prompts reflection-in-action

In a third level Open University course which I studied as a student, roughly half of the assignments were to be written in Socratic dialogue. That was also the form of presentation chosen for both the 'learning units' and for the television programmes in the study plan. Few, if any, students have ever encountered this mode of presentation in a distance learning course. Few, if any, have ever written assignments, or anything else for that matter, in the form of dialogue. Yet that mode of writing is required of them, and the choice of topic is left open to the student. This all renders more awe-inspiring the demand of the dialogue assignment, first time round.

In this context, the essence of effective dialogue is that the partner who is written into the script is rather more active in questioning than were some of the 'yes-men' who attended on Socrates himself. I vividly recall the occasion when I sat down at my PC one Sunday afternoon, to write (for my first time ever) in dialogue form. I had notes for something which I would hitherto have presented as an essay and which, if I am to be honest, I must admit I had already prepared in my mind along these lines. For the first thousand words or so, as I keyed away at my word processor, I did indeed produce an essay, loosely disguised as something in dialogue form. I had John (myself), explaining points to an attentive and dutiful Ian (my alter ego), who asked helpful questions, such as 'What then?' or 'And how do they do that?' At about 1200 words, Ian tired of this role, and began to rebel. I found that my fingers had acquired a life of their own, and suddenly had Ian challenging 'But you don't really believe it's as simple as that, do you?'

I was nonplussed. Almost beyond my control, my fingers keyed in the honest response that indeed, I did have some inner doubts about these explanations from the course materials which I was repeating, amplifying and trying to illustrate. My alter ego came back at me even more firmly. He demanded to know what I really thought – and, when I told him, he pressed me to justify that standpoint. He challenged me to grope for the truth amid the inadequacies which I felt I had encountered in the course materials and which he pressed me to acknowledge. By the time I had keyed in 2000 words, Ian was totally in charge – and John was frantically rereading the course material and reader, studying these in greater depth than ever before, in order to present something which Ian would have no option but to accept. John was now grappling with the material and the concepts on a distinctly fundamental level. Deep learning, in the Gothenburg sense (Marton *et al.*, 1984), had been prompted by the dialogue structure.

Fortunately a call to the family evening meal intervened. Even so, it was only after I had devoted Sunday evening and more time besides to a considerable amount of additional study and thinking, that John was able to recover something of his poise, and provide at least semi-adequate explanations and conclusions for Ian. The dialogue, which was by now heavily edited, reached and exceeded the word limit, with a different message from that which John would have offered in the original, (and somewhat predictable) essay-style argument he had prepared and set out to present.

Since that memorable afternoon, I have heard many other students report their own versions of that experience of mine, after their first experience of writing a dialogue assignment. It is an important learning experience. It represents for each of us a significant stage in our self-development, and has led each of us to use the dialogue format subsequently, both privately and publicly, for a variety of purposes. The dialogue format strongly encourages us to reflect-in-action on the soundness of our thinking.

Let's examine how the demand of this structure for the assignment activity led me and the others like me to follow the Kolb cycle. I had been studying in course materials of various types. In them I had encountered a theoretical input which occasioned a considerable amount of cognitive effort for me, as a learner who genuinely wished to understand. This learning and comprehension took place in the generalizing part of the Kolb diagram, although my generalizations owed a lot to the presence of many directive examples and volunteered theories within the course materials. Consequently, as I chose my central topic for my assignments, I was somewhat unwittingly preparing to test out my learning in the particular experience of the dialogue assignment.

Had I written an essay or report, I would merely have re-ordered and summarized the learning which I felt I had acquired in my dealings with the course materials. However, through the imposed structure of the dialogue and with the emergence of a partner remarkably like Karl Popper in his liking to challenge and to offer counter-examples, I was forced to reflect. I had to reflect on the validity and coherence of my learning to date, and I discovered the need to revisit some of my conclusions. I also had to explore other areas of the subject, and generally to progress and develop my generalized understanding, in the deepest sense of that word. And so, in my supplementary study which had led me on to more and deeper generalizing, I prepared to test out my further generalizations, in the particular experience of the remainder of the dialogue assignment.

No tutor had had any contact with me from the time I started to write until I had finished. So, if there was something in that turbulent educational situation which prompted me to reflect deeply and constructively, and has since prompted others similarly, it was the structure of the activity, and not the overt actions of a tutor. That structure occasioned my reflective encounter with my incomplete and inconsistent thinking; it led me, as it has led other learners on this course, to decide that something needed to be done about it; and it motivated me to take that remedial action in hand, and seek the development I desired.

Example 5.3: A letter-writing task prompts reflection-on-action

In one faculty at a British university, I encountered a commendable practice which occurred at the end of the academic year. It was used there primarily to provide feedback to the teaching staff. In a lightly structured activity, classes were brought together to generate two 'letters'. They worked first as small groups, and after that in plenary. Finally, and after full class discussion, they were able to pass on a remit to two or three writers, who would compile the final letters on their behalf.

The first of the desired epistles was to be addressed to the teachers who had planned and taught the course which the students had just completed. It was to offer advice about what these teachers should do, and should not do, in the following year. The aim was to maintain or to improve the quality of the learning and of the learning experience, and the relevance of the outcomes for the learners. The second letter was directed towards a student in the class group in the following year. This letter was to set out to be as helpful as possible to that new student. It should offer advice which would enable her or him to get the best that was possible for them from the course, to identify in advance the difficulties which would possibly or probably arise, and also to apprise them of the positive outcomes and experiences which they might expect. It also provided indirect feedback to the teachers about the learning experiences of those who had drafted the letter.

On my suggestion, several Open University tutors of my acquaintance have

followed and adapted this example with me. We have asked our students to prepare – individually – a similar pair of letters, one addressed to us as tutors, and the
other addressed to one of our next year's students. The first letter, of course, provides evaluation for the tutor – as well as constructive suggestions; in that sense it
contributes to Chapter 10, which deals with evaluation of course presentation. The
second, interestingly, changes character somewhat when it is slanted to be a letter
to a next year's student from one particular student writer, who is reflecting personally on the year that has been completed, in order to advise the other about how
to get the best possible outcome from the course, and from their learning experience. In these circumstances, I have found that the compilation of this letter,
undertaken personally and not as in the original example, tends to become a personal reflection-on-action, at the end of the academic year.

Many student writers volunteer that the assembling of such advice in the personal letter has been a most useful review experience for them. They find that it has
pushed them to reflect, and to formulate end-of-course generalizations which draw
their learning together in a way that hadn't quite happened until then. Thus a reasonably attractive, and certainly non-threatening, structure for an activity with
evaluative intent can generate overall reflection-on-action on an individual basis,
which then proves a constructive influence on further learning.

Example 5.4: Structure enhances reflection-on-and-for-action

At the end of their first term of IDS studies (Example 2.3), my first year Heriot-
Watt students, in a carefully structured activity wherein they worked with six or
seven others, were asked to draft a list of the qualities against which they would
judge their performance to date on that course. They were to prepare to appraise
their intellectual ability and their progress, in relation to the demands made by the
entire course, and in accordance with the expectations of the profession once they
would graduate. The activity was introduced by a task which encouraged students
to recall (though not necessarily to accept) one or two of the qualities which had
been instanced to them, during the term, as valued behaviour. One teacher, for
example, had made it clear that he valued students who 'identified and asked good
questions'; another had said several times that she valued 'critical thinking', without explaining what she meant by that.

The students were now free to assemble their own personal composite list, from
the group list or otherwise. They should each produce a compilation which sincerely represented their beliefs and values about the importance of the educational
outcomes, and which they would use (individually) as their own.

The students, working on their own lists, were next and individually asked to:

1. Describe what you mean by each term or heading, giving an example taken
   either from your own behaviour, or from something which you have seen someone else doing, or from something which you wish you could do, or had done;
2. Now rate yourself against this quality you have specified.

Once the students had completed and submitted this self-appraisal, they were given a photocopy of it, and asked, in their own time, to address a further task:

3. Identify in your learning journal, and in your submitted work during the past term (which has now been returned to you), the most suitable examples which you can find to endorse the claims you are making in your self-appraisal.

Most students discovered, and volunteered frankly, that their genuinely formulated self-judgement was not justified by what they could find in their own records of their performance over the previous term. They reported that they now wished to change that self-appraisal – with all the constructive implications which this reassessment, based on evaluative reflection, had for their aspirations for improvement in the second term. They next made their own plans for remedial, constructive or developmental action in the second term. Thus their generalizations, arising from reflection on the events of the first term, prompted them to form aspirations and plans for development which were soon to be worked on, in the challenges of the second term.

From the outset this was admittedly a rather devious design of both activity and structure. Students were nevertheless prompted by the format to make their own discoveries, through reflection, of mismatches between their aspirations and their perceptions of reality as evidenced in the records of their work; and to reflect for the action needed in the second term.

Facilitation through tutor intervention

Having dealt so far with examples in which the structure of the activity itself has been the catalyst for reflection, I will now describe a few examples in which tutors have a critical role, by being proactive in nudging or coercing the student into or around the Kolb cycle. This amounts to intervention during the activity, to accelerate movement by the learners through what Vygotsky (1978) called the zone of proximal development (ZPD), where something you can do 'today' with the help of somebody more experienced than you, can be something which you can do on your own, 'tomorrow'.

Example 5.5: Teachers intervene to occasion movement round the Kolb cycle

Until the course closed in 1996, all students on the Open University foundation course in mathematics (see also Example 3.1) had to attend a one-week residential summer school, which occurred roughly at the mid-point in their first year of studies. One striking feature of this summer school was a strand in the week's programme which had been elegantly designed to develop problem-solving abilities, through a range of small-group activities (Mason, 1984). In these activities, which continue nowadays in other settings, the students (who are often working as pairs), are led busily around the Kolb cycle on a number of occasions, prompted by what

I can only describe as buzz words. But the methodology is never made explicit, in terms of Kolb, to either students or tutors.

A problem is set. Perhaps the students are asked how many squares there are on a chessboard. Someone immediately volunteers the answer, 64. The tutor gently points out that there must be at least 65, because there is also the larger square which surrounds the whole board of 64 smaller squares. Convoluted, and successful and unsuccessful, discussion commences.

The tutor intervenes with the first buzz word: 'Specialize!' 'How many squares are there, for example, on a 2 × 2 chessboard?' Readily the answer of 5 emerges. 'And on a 3 × 3?' Less quickly comes the answer of 14. And so on to 4 × 4 and even a 5 × 5. As the results emerge, the tutor surreptitiously begins to prompt reflection, by summarizing the numbers in a table (Table 5.1).

Table 5.1   Tutor's summary

Size	Number of squares
1 × 1	1
2 × 2	5
3 × 3	14
4 × 4	30
5 × 5	
6 × 6	

Now it is time for the second buzz word: 'Speculate!' – followed by a sequence of prompting questions. 'Can you see a pattern in these results? Can you explain it? Can you *guess* now what the answers will be for a 6 × 6 and a 7 × 7? How did you get that?' Now it is time to move on to the third buzz word: 'Generalize!' And then more questions. 'What do you think the answer will be for an 8 × 8 – the normal chessboard? Or for a 20 × 20 chessboard? Test that out in practice, and confirm the answer, or otherwise.'

Now another buzz word: 'Rationalize!' 'Can you produce a sound explanation of the pattern of numbers which you think you have established?' And so the students move rapidly around the Kolb cycle, so quickly that they almost go straight back and forward from particular examples to generalizations (or at least the assembly of data which leads to generalization), being rushed somewhat quickly through reflection into generalization, and then from generalization, back through the planning to test it, to a more demanding particular example.

The pattern continues, with more and more complex problems. In every case the students are encouraged to simplify the problem first of all to an easily solved form. One such problem describes the familiar case of the man searching in the dark for socks, in a drawer which contains many individual socks of several colours. The tutor suggests that the students should first reduce the number of colours in the drawer to two – and next perhaps to work out what happens if there are three colours, and so on. But once the generalization has been assembled and rationalized, the tutor will urge that they should test out their conclusion on something which is even more complex than the stated problem. What happens if the socks are being obtained for a four-legged pet, and if there are five colours of socks available in the drawer? And so on to a centipede seeking to be properly dressed from a drawer containing fifteen, or more, colours of socks.

The tutor's role in all of this is simply to urge the students, just when they have begun to become comfortable in the pattern of dealing with particular cases, to move from particular examples of *experience* through quick and almost natural *reflection* to *generalizing*. And, similarly, the tutor coaxes them from generalizing to *testing* on a more complex particular example, just as they have begun to be comfortable with their generalizing. The tutor is an intervening facilitator, albeit someone who does that in a gentle and encouraging way, and even with humour. Nevertheless the tutor's interventions are not always welcomed by the students, who prefer to settle into a pattern of thinking at any one point in the cycle which, when it becomes settled and seductively comfortable, also becomes relatively undemanding and, more importantly, less productive.

In the days of the mathematics summer school, the programme commenced with a demonstration in plenary to about 100–200 students in a lecture theatre. There a course director, working from the front, introduced both the ideas and the buzz words in one or two opening examples. This 'master tutor' gently coaxed the entire class to work with him or her, in the manner I have described, through the first of the many problems which the students were to encounter in the plenary. Thereafter the tutors who were to be facilitative worked with small groups of about 12 students. Some of these tutors had not worked with this activity or in this way. They found that they could readily assimilate from this demonstration what was required of them, and could perform effectively in that role on their first attempt – urging the students to move swiftly from specializing to speculating, or from speculating to generalizing.

The outcome was that, at a later stage in the week's programme, students successfully, and independently of tutor support, tackled one demanding problem for an assignment where half of the marks were for a reflective analysis of the process which they had followed, and only half for the extent to which they obtained an adequate solution.

I suggest to you that the significant features in this example – for the tutor, and for the tutoring – are that:

- the stewardship of the pedagogy is vested in the tutor;
- the tutor actively intervenes to prompt cycling according to Kolb;
- the tutor works deliberately to bring about frequent cycles, in quick succession, around the Kolb diagram;
- there is increasing awareness, on the part of the students, of the process they are following;
- there is a natural reluctance on the part of the learners to move on round the Kolb cycle, which is overcome by the proactive interventions of the tutors.

Example 5.6: Tutors intervene to occasion reflection-in-action

I presented my first year Heriot-Watt students with a problem situation, and asked them to respond to it by designing and constructing a model structure made from balsawood and glue, or spaghetti and adhesive tape. I might call for a tower, a bridge or a cantilever. Before starting the task, I asked the groups to sit down and summarize, step by step, the process which they would follow while analysing the problem, and in formulating a number of distinct and competitive responses to it, until they could eventually choose which one to work through in detail, as their favoured design. At the outset, the groups spent little time on this part of the activity. The descriptions of the design process which were produced, and which were set out on flipchart sheets behind the area in which each group was working, were sparse in detail, thoughtless and often inaccurate in wording.

This modelling activity was competitive, and motivating. Hence the groups were understandably keen to get on to the practical work. They wanted to decide on a design, to fabricate it, to test it tentatively, and as quickly as possible to enter the arena in which their model might gain the maximum possible marks by sustaining a greater load before failure than any of the others. In this setting there was, however, one disruptive rule of the game. This was that any peripatetic tutor, wandering round the groups and observing their processes, might challenge any group at any time – if the description of the process which they were supposed to be following, as it was displayed on the flipchart behind them, did not conform with what the tutor observed them to be doing. If that proved to be so, the students had to stop in their designing and fabricating activity, and had to rewrite a more accurate statement of the process in which they were now engaged, in sufficient detail to satisfy the tutor. A similar challenge could be made if the process was not sufficiently detailed on the flipchart sheet; the group accordingly had to amplify, so that their description was reasonably comprehensive and informative.

There was naturally much frustration on the part of the students when they were interrupted. They found it difficult to see the point of these interventions. After all, they knew what they were setting out to do, and how they intended to achieve it – so why should they bother recording that, in pedantic detail, on a flipchart sheet?

I tried out this activity, with and without the declaration and amendment of the design process on flipchart sheets. Matched groups were pre-tested and post-tested (see Example 10.1). It was thus possible for me to compare results and to demonstrate that performance in designing effective model structures improved with concentration on, and awareness of, process; and that, if groups were left undisturbed by tutor interventions, their performance did not improve to the same extent as it did when reflection on process was required, in the manner I have described.

At that early stage in their studies, the students had yet to acquire the ability to describe the process which they follow when they are designing an artefact. Their descriptions tended to be vague, and too general to be useful. More importantly, they were often inaccurate – the rhetoric being distinct from the reality. Interventions which prompted reflection-in-action focused attention on this weakness.

There is a school of thought which claims to show that awareness of process goes hand in hand with the ability to execute that process and to improve it. That is why it seemed useful for tutors to intervene – to encourage students to reflect by ensuring that they articulate, in general terms, what they are doing; and that they scrutinize what they actually do, in order to decide if their general description needs to be revised. In other words, it is potentially creative to construct, in a particular situation, something of a dialogue between the description of process and the reality of process – a dialogue which, in effect, implies rapid circulation around the Kolb cycle and hence reflection-in-action. That reflective interaction was occasioned in this example by the tutors' interventions during the activity, more than by the structure of the task.

Example 5.7: A teacher intervenes by providing an input

My first year Heriot-Watt students followed a programme which contained a wide assortment of group activities. One of the goals of the first year IDS programme (Example 2.3) was therefore to help the students to develop the interpersonal skills which could contribute to effective group working. And so the groups which met on the Tuesday afternoons and on the Wednesday mornings were often treated as 'home' groups, having been chosen so that they did not contain any two students who had been working together in other groups during the remainder of the week.

In these activities dealing with interpersonal skills, the students were often provided with an input (as usual in the form of an example demonstrated by their tutors). This input might exemplify a methodology for observing, analysing or understanding their behaviour as people in groups. An example of this, from an early week in the programme, was the introduction of the basic methods and vocabulary of transactional analysis. This was done through simple reporting of an analysis of transactions which the tutors had drawn up, recently and unobtrusively, as they observed groups working within the class programme.

In their first exploration of such an input, the students followed it through to study their own behaviour within a brief and somewhat artificially contrived activity involving the home group. Having grasped a method of enquiry or a theoretical explanation of behaviour, they proceeded to apply it to some of the group activities with which they had been engaged in the previous week or ten days. On that basis, they went on to reflect constructively on means of rendering more effective and productive the group working in which they would be engaged in the week ahead.

As the teacher, I had felt that I needed to provide a significant theoretical input which could be put to good use. I thought it ineffective and almost irresponsible to leave the students to analyse experience without a basis on which to do so. Thus I started the students' progress round the Kolb cycle with a generalization to be tested out – first on a particular experience which was contrived for them, and then on experiences which occurred naturally in the course of their studies in groups. The students reflected on all of that, thus consolidating their understanding of the theory or generalization; and then they applied that method of analysis to other recent experiences, taken from a variety of current group-working situations.

The significant features of this example appear to me to be that:

- the cycling began at a different point in the cycle from that of Example 5.6;
- a tutor intervened to make a powerful input at the generalization part of the Kolb cycle, in order to arm the students to test this out in a forthcoming experience or set of experiences;
- the students accepted that tutors could act in that way;
- the input was both a method of enquiry and a conceptual framework;
- the outcome was deep and informed reflection-on-action.

Example 5.8: Tutors provoke reflection by offering examples

In the Open University in Scotland, we had long identified and discussed the need to develop the transferable competences which are used in the study of science at second level. I was associated, for a number of years, with workshop programmes which had that objective. They began with a structured reflection on past experiences. We asked students to reflect on the various demands placed on them by their studies in science at second level, and first to identify and next to detail the skills or competences which they had had to use.

Even with these somewhat elementary goals, our activities proved disappointing. For they merely generated two types of regrettably shallow output which were both an inadequate foundation for further development. The first outcome was a list of tentatively described study skills of a very basic nature; this was relatively unhelpful because it would have been equally applicable to foundation level study, or even to studies in school. The second common outcome was an assortment of distinctly vague headings such as 'organizing' or 'problem-solving'. That again did not do much to establish a starting point from which effective reflection and generalization might proceed.

I aspired to rise above this failure on my part to create an effective context for reflection. I chose to work with several science tutors. We set out to give an effective introduction to the reformulated task. We demonstrated how we wanted the students to proceed by first providing our own listing of descriptive examples of skills which we had found that we ourselves used in science and technology; but we had carefully chosen our examples to be inappropriate to their student experiences. For instance, the tutors cited such examples as:

- noticing what is not there;
- finding the solution to a design problem from within the analysis of the brief;
- deciding whether or not to rely on a published research paper which appears useful.

We were joining the students, in effect, in their zone of proximal development (Vygotsky, 1978). After tabling a short list of examples like that, from our own experiences of studying and learning (which was not necessarily in science), we asked gently but (I hope) facilitatively, 'Is that what *you* have to do, in *your* studies of science?' And then, when this question in turn produced the (expected) negative response, we asked 'What *do* you have to do, then?' The end result of this was an excellent list of suggestions, rich both in quantity and in quality. Geddes and Wood (1995) have given examples of the abilities which have figured in the lists produced for them, in these circumstances, by a small group of science students.

Thus we discovered, or rather confirmed, my impression that a poor response to a task of this nature can arise because the task is not clearly understood or grasped, or is not effectively facilitated – and not because the students lack the experience or the ability to identify what is required. We also showed, to our own satisfaction at least, that an input from tutors who illustrate what they mean by the analysing of experience can be usefully explanatory, provocative, non-directive and surely necessary – provided it does not overlap with the students' analyses of their own experiences.

Example 5.9: A structured intervention provokes reflection-on-action

This example centres on a student of second level science, who came to a personal tutorial with three genuine enquiries in mind. The consultation, which was one-to-one, took place, by arrangement, in a room where there was a video camera focused on the tutor. Recording commenced just before the tutorial exchange began.

The student posed her first question or difficulty. The tutor and the student worked on this together, in the usual manner, until it appeared to the tutor that the difficulty had been resolved. At this point the tutor awaited the student's endorsement of that judgement. The tutor expected an indication that the student was ready to move on to the second problem or difficulty. The conversation quickly became somewhat hesitant and sticky.

(I will interrupt my description of the tutorial exchange at this point, because now I wish to explain the reason for allowing the television camera to intrude. This experiment concerned an adaptation by me (Cowan and George, 1992a) of a process called Interpersonal Process Recall (IPR), devised originally for an entirely different purpose by a counsellor called Kagan (Kagan *et al.*, 1963). I have been employing this technique over the past ten or fifteen years, to extract recall of thoughts and feelings, as they have occurred in the minds of learners and tutors at the time of their dialogues together.)

Here is how IPR was used in this particular example. A colleague of the tutor, acting as an enquirer, went with the student to a separate room, where there was a replay facility. Enquirer and tutor between them had selected three or four minutes of the exchange which appeared to the tutor to be likely to be of interest, and worth exploring in detail. The student, who knew in advance of the technique and how it would be employed, was reminded that the question asked of her would always be the same, each time the tape was paused: 'Does that remind you of how you were thinking or feeling at the time?' After her reply, there might be further questions of elucidation, seeking simply to amplify her original answer.

(In all my experience of the use of this technique, those who have not experienced it before have always found it an exciting revelation. For they discover the extent to which they can have access to what virtually amounts to a replay of their thoughts and feelings. These impressions come back from memory in sharp detail which the subjects would never have imagined possible. They thus provide information which subjects could certainly not have been able to recall without the prompt of the recording.)

In this instance, the tutor naturally chose the four-minute section of the recording which covered the end of the dialogue around the first difficulty, and the hiatus which occurred thereafter. Although it was the student's thoughts and feelings which were 'unpacked' first of all, it will make my point more effectively if I first describe what the enquirer extracted from the tutor.

The tutor felt sure that something had gone wrong – but he did not know what. The tutor was perturbed by the look on the student's face, and by the student's reluctance to speak, to answer, to table the next difficulty, or – generally – to respond. The replay was stopped, either at an appropriate break or because the tutor's eye movement as he watched the replay suggested to the enquirer that important recall was occurring. Each time this tutor recalled vividly the anxiety he had been feeling, and his various frantic speculations about what he might have done wrong. Eventually he progressed to recall his clear judgement at the time, which was that the student wished the exchange to end as soon as possible, and that he, the tutor, should quickly find a way of allowing the student to terminate the appointment without further embarrassment on either side.

The student's recall, which the enquirer had obtained earlier but had not declared at this point to the tutor, followed rather different lines. Her facial signals had led the enquirer to stop the tape frequently, at almost 15 second intervals. This staccato replay of the tape had prompted her to recall (first) her satisfaction that her difficulty had been resolved, and (subsequently) her consciousness that her new understanding now began to answer a lot of associated difficulties which had occurred in the previous week or ten days. She had begun to think these through – as she was then recalling in detail. She remembered – also vividly – her anxiety not to lose that which she felt she had just begun to grasp, her acute need for time to think all of this through again, and above all her fervent hope that the tutor would just stay silent for a minute or two, leaving her to tidy all of this away before moving on to her next question.

Here we have a classic example of one of those mismatches in perception between a tutor and a student (or a group of students) which are a common discovery in IPR enquiries. When this student and her tutor came together to hear the reports from the enquirer, both were adult learners, and both were learning in their different ways, and to their surprise, about the process of learning and teaching. The student learned that her facial expressions and her silences could be misread by at least one tutor. She eventually began to discuss, and see the desirability of, feeding back information to a tutor about the immediate outcomes of tutoring. The tutor, in his turn, learned to his horror how badly he had misjudged the facial expressions and behaviour of the student, and particularly the reasons for the student's reticence. He saw the need to develop for the future a tutorial style in which silences might figure rather more often, and without unease on his part. He would also devise and use more effective questions than hitherto, in order to ascertain the process of the learning which was occurring in response to his teaching; and he planned to introduce that suggestion in future, by a brief reference to this particular experience. Thus, from this relatively brief experience, both went off resolved to test out the tentative conclusions of their deep and fairly lengthy discussion on process, and to do so in the next tutorial exchanges in which they were engaged.

Student and tutor, as I have described, began from a particular experience of teaching or learning; they each progressed through extensive reflection which they undertook together after it had been occasioned by the prompting of the feedback from the enquirer. They next moved into tentative generalizations about teaching and learning, which each was immediately eager to test out or verify in practice, in the next similar, but hopefully now also dissimilar, situation.

The significant features of this interaction, in terms of what the facilitator had planned, were that:

- The facilitator, in effect, arranged in advance for intervention immediately after the event, in order to bring about, or at least prompt, powerful reflection – without, in the event, even being present.
- He did this by arranging for the use of a proven technique which – by that point in time – had become fairly standard in the institution in which it was once again being used.
- The enquirer's only intervention was to stop the tape replay when the subject's face suggested that significant recall was happening; to ask, if necessary, the same prompt question; to follow up that question, when appropriate, with simple questions of elucidation; and to note the information volunteered, and pass it on to the tutor, and vice versa.
- There was no active facilitation of the reflection itself, but only the creation of occasions for reflection.
- The reflection led (for the tutor) to an awareness of misconception of self which was somewhat negative in the first instance; it was only later that a generalization of a positive or constructive nature was to emerge.

Other examples

- The reflection in Example 2.1 (Study skills for OU students at Dumfries) depended on the structure of the activity.
- The reflection in Example 2.2 (Identifying and using algorithms in applied mechanics) also depended on the structure of the activity.
- The Aalborg supervisors, in Example 2.4, intervene throughout the progress of the projects, and especially to require review and reflection.

Possible non-examples

- Woods (1987), who is one of the gurus of problem-solving education, explicitly declares his specific problem-solving methods to students, and teaches them almost by instruction.

- Rogers (1983) advises against the structuring of activity or of intervention by the teacher, who is to be empathic and responsive.
- The journal commentators in Example 2.3 (the Interdisciplinary Studies course) did not impose structure although they actively (if non-directively) provided comments which the journal writers might accept as facilitation of further reflection. (Is this a non-example, then?)

Generalizations

A number of noteworthy features emerge, for me at least, from my nine examples. It may be helpful to declare them to you, as a reader who seeks an answer to the question at the head of this chapter. My thoughts include, but are not restricted to, the following:

- The designer of each activity had a clear notion of the intended outcome, and chose an arrangement which, if successful, should have achieved that outcome.
- The demands made on the learners were fairly straightforward, at least in terms of the explanation or description of their task.
- Where the structure of the activity could be made to achieve the desired purpose, minimal tutor engagement was incorporated, other than to describe to the students what was to be done.
- The structures chosen were such that good (or better) practice should have ensued for the learners, or were such that ineffective practice would become apparent.
- On occasions, and in some activities only, success apparently depended heavily on interventions by the tutor, to nudge learners around the Kolb cycle.
- The tutors did not attempt to instruct the students in the exercise of the ability which was the focus of the activity.
- The more learners had autonomy over the outcomes of learning, the more tutors appeared to take responsibility for the *structure* of the learning activity. Tutors also, consequently, gave more thought to these issues, including their roles within teaching and learning situations.

Before you test this, some second thoughts from me

1. Is it a valid reflective summary to conclude that it is through the design of the structure of an activity or programme that the teacher sets in place the Kolb cycle, or the potential to follow it? And is it by facilitative interventions or interactions that the teacher will most effectively encourage constructive progress around that cycle?
2. Demanding structures and powerful interventions can be threatening and will then inhibit instead of nurturing worthwhile learning and development. How can teachers judge in advance how far they can go in the search for methods and approaches to develop learners' potential to the full?

3. The human race progresses because we build on the experience and learning of those who went before us. So should it not have been possible, as well as desirable for the sake of efficient use of the time of all concerned, to condense the experience of those who went before the learners in the examples described in this chapter, and thus to expedite the learners' progress? Couldn't learners have been taken directly to the generalizations? I have been urging you to form your own generalizations from the examples I offer you. Are these generalizations genuinely 'better', according to criteria for *your* development which you value, than they would have been if I had gone straight into an exposition of my approach to the development of abilities, and only then justified it by quoting examples – while still leaving you to decide if you were convinced? What place is there, even in reflective learning, for the teacher who instructs and directs – rather than structuring and intervening? Surely these options, like many in this book, are not mutually exclusive?

4. You will undoubtedly have recognized that, as the writer of this text, I am an example of a teacher who has opted to make substantial inputs to his readers. I have clearly had a devious intent from the outset, stemming from a clear decision about the view I wish to 'sell' to you, and to other readers. My many examples appear to be simply a way of presenting my view and my preferred approach to teaching and learning, with only one intended conclusion – if you follow me through the reflections I have structured for you, and into the generalizations which I have in mind for you. Are you genuinely free to generalize, and decide how to do that, in your own ways? *Should* you be? Is it acceptable for a facilitative tutor to have intended outcomes in mind?

A final thought

Finally, I offer a long-standing reflection on the diminishing role of a true teacher:

> The whole function of the teacher is epitomized in two sayings from the Fourth Gospel: 'I have come that men may have life, and may have it in all its fullness' (John 10; 10) and 'It is for your good that I am leaving you' (John 16; 7).
>
> (paraphrased from H.G. Stead, in Davies, 1971)

Dear John

You spoke in your last notes to me about two kinds of reflection, but since then you seem to have let that distinction slip.

    I would like you to go back to your distinction between analytical and evaluative reflection, because I didn't really follow what you meant by that comment. Surely all reflection must be analytical? For the learner, or at least a learner following your Kolb cycle, must analyse the particular experiences in an attempt to make generalizable sense out of them.

    Please let's not get too deeply into any philosophical or pedagogical discussions. Just concentrate on explaining to me what analytical reflection might involve for my students (and for me), if I decide to follow in your footsteps.

6

What is Involved for Students in Analytical Reflection?

Introduction

In this chapter I offer six examples, which I hope are of some intrinsic interest in their own right as modest innovations in education. They also exemplify, I believe, reflection which leads to learning, and is analytic. For further examples I refer back to earlier chapters in this book; and for non-examples, forward to Chapter 7, which you have yet to read. My generalizations and second thoughts are present but are rather briefer than usual.

Example 6.1: Reflective analysis of processes

We had been given a report to write, for Properties and Use of Materials. We had to find an example of something which had been built by a civil engineer, and which was damaged – in a way which didn't make it immediately obvious what had caused the damage. A crumpled building with a double decker bus embedded in the front wall wouldn't do. In our report, we had to describe both the building, and the damage we had seen in it. Finally we had to present our diagnosis of the cause of damage, and justify that judgement. The report had to be written in two sections, which were to be on separate pieces of paper, for some reason which we didn't follow straightaway.

We were offered the opportunity of what our lecturer called a cooperative workshop. We were told that we would be admitted to this workshop if we had completed a reasonably thorough draft of our report. If we hadn't done that properly, or if we hadn't even started it, we were turned back at the door of the seminar room – and sent to the library, to use our time sensibly, in catching up. I was all right, though; I could show that I had a complete report in draft – so I was welcomed to the workshop.

We were put into groups of five or six students. The lecturer collected our reports, and passed them to another group, some distance away. Our group got the bundle of reports from a group at the other side of the room – we weren't quite sure which group that was, but it didn't matter anyway. We read each draft, and chose one of them to begin on. We had to suggest ways in which each report could be improved. The plan for the activity helped us to do that. This plan told us that we should first look only at the descriptions, and work out what we ourselves thought was the cause of the damage, and also note any information which we thought we lacked. Sometimes we felt that the writer could usefully have told us more. This part of the activity made us think about how best to describe things.

We often disagreed amongst ourselves about what we thought had happened to cause damage. We had to discuss our various possible diagnoses thoroughly, but we didn't have to reach agreement. After that discussion, we were to check over the writer's diagnosis on the second sheet – and often we found that we disagreed with that, as well. This made us think really hard about our reasoning. Often we found weaknesses in it. This part of the exercise made us think about how to put together a good argument.

The lecturer also told us that, when we had read the writer's diagnosis, we should next try to predict all the consequences which should be seen in the building, if that diagnosis was correct. Often we didn't find all of the outcomes that we predicted. Again, that made us rethink and reconsider – about the writer's diagnosis, and about ours, and about how we had reached our one.

For instance, our group was given a description of a large house with a whole lot of cracks in it, in one wall which faced a garden area. There were a number of rapidly growing trees in the garden. Some of these were quite near the house. Three of us in the group thought that the cracks were due to the growth of the larger trees in the garden area. Two others noticed, from a photograph in the report, that there was a lot of staining and mould on the face of the wall. They felt that there must have been some chemical action, which had maybe made parts of the wall swell or shrink, while other parts hadn't been affected. But the writer of the report put it all down to subsidence – without saying what had caused the subsidence. When we thought about the effects which subsidence would have had on this house, one of our group pointed out that, if you looked along the brick wall of the building, the horizontal bed lines shouldn't be straight and level any more. We looked at a photograph which was in the report, and the lines seemed to be straight. That made it difficult to agree with the diagnosis of subsidence as the cause of cracking. It also made us more critical of our own diagnoses of the cause of cracking, and so we asked ourselves more questions about our conclusions. Now we were having to think about everything that can go wrong when you make up a diagnosis – and, the other way round, what *we* should do to diagnose well.

We weren't supposed to do the job of the writer of the report, for him or her. We didn't have to find or justify our diagnosis of the cause of failure. We just had to point out ways in which the report, and especially the reasoning in it, was unconvincing or incomplete, and how it might be improved. Sometimes, for instance, the description didn't tell us all that we had wanted to know, or it seemed to be illogical. In either case, that was worth reporting back. The writer could stick to the original diagnosis, improve the description, or even change the argument for the diagnosis. That was their decision.

After all of this, I didn't really need to get my own report back in order to appreciate what had to be done to improve it. I had already seen lots of things wrong with the reports that we worked on, when they were discussed in our group. And I had often found myself thinking immediately that the same criticism would apply to my own report. So I knew what I was going to be told, before my draft came back to me. In fact, I had one or two extra suggestions of my own, which the group who looked at my report didn't pick up.

Next time I write a report of this type, I'll be better able to put my argument together – and to present it. Because – by looking at reports that weren't well enough done – this activity made me think. I thought about how to describe structures, and how to put together convincing arguments, and get to a diagnosis. I'll do all of these things better next time, whatever they ask me to do.

That last paragraph sums it up, doesn't it? The nature of the task called on these students to scrutinize descriptions, to analyse the coherence of the descriptions and arguments presented by their fellow students, to reflect on these analyses and to learn from them. From the particular examples before them, they moved through their analytical reflection to a developing and generalized appreciation of what makes adequate describing and satisfactory explaining.

Example 6.2: Thinking about thinking – and thinking about thinking about thinking!

(See Example 2.3)

I was writing in my learning journal, near the end of my first year of studies in IDS. This made me look back over the year. I found myself thinking what a change there had been in me as a result of keeping a learning journal.

Mind you, I hated doing it at first. I didn't see the point, I couldn't write anything sensible, and I was really worried at first about what the lecturer would comment when my dreadful mess of a journal entry went in each week. But, as the weeks have gone past, I have found to my relief that the lecturer doesn't criticize what I've written. I've also begun to acquire the habit of mulling over the week that is past. So it's easier to write nowadays – and more useful, too.

Do you know, it's curious. Sometimes when I sit at my desk at home, either working on course materials or writing up my journals, it's as if a ghost came out of me, and stood behind my shoulder, and offered me advice about how to be more effective in the things I have to do in my studies. If I'm working on engineering or science subjects, it could be advice about how to tackle the studying or the problems on the tutorial sheets. If I'm writing my journal, it could be prompting thoughts – before I write anything down – about what I should be saying in it, or thinking about.

And sometimes, though it makes me feel foolish to admit this, it's almost as if a second ghost came out of the first ghost, and offered advice to the first ghost about how to offer me advice. Can you understand what I mean by that?

I can certainly warm to this student's account. It reminds me powerfully of a paper by the Cambridge researcher, Pask (1975), who presented a delightful image of the thinking about thinking which educationists call metacognition. He pictures the student, or anyone else who is tackling a problem or a challenge, as being like an animal in a maze, seeking the best way out. Somehow, from that animal, there emerges a thoughtful part – which climbs up a ladder near the maze, to an observation platform. Sitting on the platform, the thoughtful part of the problem-solving animal watches what is happening, sees where it is going wrong and how it might be improved, and offers advice to the problem-solving part of the animal, down there in the maze – advice about how to do better, and indeed about what to do.

And sometimes, Pask tells us, there can be another thoughtful part which emerges in turn from the observer on the platform. This one climbs up a further stage in the ladder to a higher platform, to offer advice to the observer on the first platform – about how to be a more purposeful and useful observer.

At no time in his studies, or from his contacts with me and my colleagues, did the student whose account we have just read encounter Pask's wonderful picture of metacognition, and indeed of that meta-metacognition which occurs when the observer on the second platform (or the second ghost) is proactively involved. The week-by-week experience of reflective and analytical journalling, coupled with the facilitative comments from a tutor, led a relatively undistinguished first year student of civil engineering to this rather splendid journal entry – which I still keep, and still treasure. I would argue that two and a half terms of facilitated self-analysis and reflection led him to this discovery which, being new for him, was a great achievement, and represented truly deep metacognitive learning and development.

Example 6.3: Time out – for reflective analysis of process-in-action

In 1991 my colleague, Judith George, went to Alverno College in Milwaukee as a student. She lived as a student, socialized little with the staff, and took part as a student in all the classes where she participated.

In one such class, the tutor wished the students to explore four different ways of analysing a piece of literature. She divided the class into four similar groups. She explained to each group an emphasis on which she wished them to concentrate in their literary analysis. It was her intention that, in due course, each group would report back in plenary to the other three groups, with both their findings and their thoughts about their assigned analytical emphasis. Notice, then, that – typically for Alverno – there was as much emphasis on process awareness and development as on rigorous content coverage.

The small-group activities began, and went well for a while – or, at least, they went well for three of the groups. The fourth group, however, encountered considerable difficulties. They just weren't able to get going; and none of them could put a finger on what had gone wrong. In characteristically supportive Alverno fashion, someone in one of the other groups noticed this and quickly enquired what was happening, or rather what was not happening. When she confirmed that the fourth group were having difficulties, she called 'Time out!' to the rest of the class.

The plenary reconvened, with the group tasks set aside for the moment. The entire class, without the involvement of the tutor, began to address the problem of the group with difficulties. They didn't try to work on the task which the struggling group had been given. What they did do was to try to find out why that group were having difficulty with a task of this type, when the three other groups in the room had managed to cope with their own particular emphasis in analysis, in their particular situations. The whole class spent some time on constructive discussion, suggestions, questions and, above all, analytical sharing of experiences – which were experiences of process, and not yet of outcomes. Soon the group with difficulties felt sufficiently in command of the processes which had been shared with them to propose that the other three groups should return to their own tasks, leaving the fourth group, who were now able to proceed, to do so on their own.

This is an interesting example, which arose because there were four similar, but distinct, experiences progressing within one class at the same time. When one of these encountered difficulties, the students from the other three groups volunteered to pool their experiences. Through analytical reflection on the processes being followed, the class as a whole attempted to distil that which was common to the three successful groups, for the benefit of the fourth group. The fourth group, in turn, detached themselves from the immediate frustrations of a process which was not going well for them, and attempted in their own way to analyse what it was that they had been doing. It was by comparing that experience in the full class with what the others had been doing, that the students in the fourth group found enough of a solution from the analytical generalization which thereby emerged, and felt confident to test this out on returning to their own particular task.

Comment

Tasks, once understood and mastered, tend to be perceived and summarized by competent learners in generalized terms (as in Examples 2.1 and 2.2). But, before mastery is achieved, and especially where a generalized method or process is not grasped, learners or problem-solvers tend to see a task only as a particular challenge. Through analytical reflection which concentrates on (and brings out, and reinforces) the generalities, learners can be enabled to proceed from a tentative and particular experience to the generalized grasp which is associated with the ability to tackle a range of tasks of a given type.

Example 6.4: Reflective analysis which identified – and met – needs

I don't know anything about Kelly's Repertory Grid. I understand that it was the research method used in the experience I have to report. I'll just tell you how it appeared to me.

I am an Open University student. In the year I've been asked to tell you about, I was studying the Foundation Course in social sciences. My tutor approached all of the students in her group, asking us if we would take part in a study which she hoped would enable her to offer us better correspondence tuition. She told us what she wanted us to do – which sounded fairly straight-forward. So I agreed to cooperate.

In the Open University, when we send in assignments, the tutor marks these and sends them to Milton Keynes. They are posted back to us a few days later. In this project, it was to be rather different. The tutor had arranged for a colleague to bring my assignment, when she had marked it, straight back to me – like a postman. This man phoned to tell me when he would be coming to see me. He told me that I was to open the envelope, read the comments and think about them, in just the same way as I usually do when the real postman pops a letter from Milton Keynes through my letter box.

The assignment came back to me somewhat earlier than usual. After I had read it, the postman-tutor explained in detail what I had to do. He gave me an example of three types of 'street furniture', as he called it – traffic lights, a bus stop and a lamp post. And he asked me to divide these into a pair and a single-ton, in a way that seemed meaningful to me, according to the fact that they were items of street furniture. In other words, he said, I wasn't to use the fact that the bus stop and the lamp post had a lot in common, because in each case the second word began with the last letter of the first word. That wasn't really an important distinction for street furniture, he said. I agreed.

I chose to go for the two which stopped vehicles – the bus stop and the traf-fic lights. He said that this was a good response. He told me that it would have been equally valid to separate out the two which required electricity. For, he explained, in each case we would have found out something important about street furniture. The effect which something has on the flow of traffic is important; and the need (or not) for a supply of electricity is also relevant.

He then took me to the comments on my assignment, which I had been warned would be numbered by my tutor. He told me that he wanted me to divide groups of three comments into a pair, and a singleton. He asked me to look at comments 1, 2 and 3 – and remind myself of what they said, and of how I had reacted when I had read them. He asked me to divide them into a pair and a singleton, according to a category or feature which was meaningful to me, either in terms of the type of comments that I thought they were, or my reactions to them. I chose to separate out comment 2 from comments 1 and 3. Comments 1 and 3 told me that I had done something well; but comment 2 told me that I had missed something out. He now asked me to go through all the other comments, picking out those which told me I had done something well. He ticked these on his sheet, and crossed the others.

When I had done that, he picked a further three numbers, for comments which had all told me I had done well – and again asked me to subdivide. That was more difficult. However in the trio that he chose, one comment explained what it was that I had done well, which was useful – and I was glad to be told what was good; and the other two didn't explain, so I had felt a bit frustrated, even though I had apparently written something which was OK. So I divided them on that basis.

We went on doing this several times, always starting with a trio which I had categorized in the same way up till then – until he ran out of available trios. At that point, he checked out with me the various features or characteristics which I had been telling him about. He asked me if there were any other features of the comments on my assignments which mattered to me. I thought of two more to mention. One of them, I remember, was whether or not the comment was a surprise to me. We went down the list of comments and categorized them again, according to each of my two additional headings.

Finally, he asked me to tell my tutor, through him, about what type of comment I found most useful, and why. I chose the type of comment which told me that I had 'done something well because . . .'. I find this more helpful than simply being told what it is that I have done well. Because I need to know what made it a good part of the assignment.

I found this a surprisingly interesting and useful experience, because it made me realize what it is that I am doing, and especially what I hope to find, when I read my tutor's comments on my assignment. The piece of learning in the assignment is by then away in the past. By the time the assignment comes back, I'm usually about three weeks further on in my studies than I was when I wrote it – or at least when I began to write it. So I'm on to something new.

That's why the comments which are most useful to me (at least until we get to exam revision time!) are those which give me an idea about the kind of thing that they want me to do, and how they want me to do it. Now I can see clearly that I make most use of comments about the things which work well and matter in this subject that I am studying, and comments about how well I am doing, so that I can plan for next time. I can't get all of that from the marks alone, and I can't quite predict it when I write my assignments.

Through an analytical activity which had primarily been planned to provide information for the tutor about the effect and effectiveness of her comments on assignments, this student (and others) developed a better awareness of how to use, and respond to, tutorial comments. This happened partly because she was urged to differentiate between comments in an analytical way, with the result that she could reflect on what mattered to her in them; and partly because she had the real opportunity to send back an informative message to her tutor, and influence the tutor–learner relationship and her subsequent correspondence tuition accordingly.

The student learned through analytic reflection to identify what it is in the tutor–student interchange which is useful to her; and she found – or would soon discover – that it is profitable to report this back to her tutor. Perhaps we leave too much responsibility with the teaching person for the nature and quality of the teacher–learner exchange. Perhaps this should be a joint responsibility, just as it is a joint relationship. If so, an analytical reflection of the type described (Weedon, 1994) can lead to an informed communication from the learner to the tutor. That can be a valuable part of the discharge of the learner's responsibility and may lead constructively to improvement in the learning experience.

Example 6.5: Reflective analysis of values in a discipline

After years of studying in the social sciences, I decided to study the Open University course A295: *Homer, Poetry and Society*. This is an intriguing multidisciplinary course, which provides a mass of resource material and ideas. It also offers a difficult challenge when, after two moderately standard essay-type assignments, the pattern changes. The third assignment called on me to design my own assignment question and to plan the way I would tackle it; and the fourth expected me to respond accordingly, and then to review the process and the final plan that I had actually followed.

I had been intrigued by a suggestion in one of the papers given in the course reader. The writer argued that peasant societies have behaved similarly throughout the ages, in encouraging their members to tell lies; and he maintained that they have all regarded dishonesty as normal, and even praiseworthy, behaviour. This key paper developed that argument, relating it to the lying tales told by Odysseus, and justifying it by reference to a number of research papers about ethnographic studies of Greek peasant village cultures of the twentieth century. These papers appeared to have been translated into English.

I already knew from my holiday reading of the existence of highly rated peasant literature from the Irish-speaking community and oral tradition of the Blasket Islands, off the south-west coast of Ireland. This was a community where, from my vague memories of the English version of the texts, I recalled little evidence of the dishonesty associated with Odysseus, and attributed to all peasant societies by the writer whom I felt I wished to challenge. In addition, I found the argument in the paper in the reader somewhat ragged – and I wondered how sound I would find it, if I went back to the original sources.

I tried to formulate an assignment task based on these vague worries. I had to carry out a great deal of carefully directed searching and reading, linked to an ongoing analysis of what was emerging from these tentative explorations. I found that I now knew my subject matter better, and more deeply, than when I had started out on this assignment task.

Or did I? The more I wrestled with the design of my final assignment question, the more I realized that I had to think through what 'satisfactory' meant in this strange new discipline of Arts. If I didn't sort that one out, how could I produce a satisfactory piece of work, or better? I went back to the course units, the study guide and the assignment notes – and to my tutor's comments on those first two assignments. It became apparent to me that what they had valued in my previous studies in social sciences, was not the same as what they valued in Arts. Having come recently from that social sciences background, I felt like a stranger trying to be accepted in a different cultural village. So, in order to design an adequate task and answer it satisfactorily or better, I had to analyse what I believe some people have called the 'nature of discourse' in this discipline of Arts and, in particular, in classical studies.

In other words, starting from a point of interest, and one or two ideas for reading, I found myself pushed by the task which had been set for me, to reflect analytically on the type of question and style of response which would be adequate in this discipline. And then I had to work out how I myself could study, think and write with such goals, while answering that question.

In the final assignment, I had to review the process I had followed to get through the formulation of a question, the assembling of an answer, and the judging of what would make a good answer. It was only then that I began to realize that this assignment hadn't been about Homer; it had been about learning to learn.

There are strong echoes there of a declaration by Carl Rogers (1969), who maintained that the most socially useful learning in the modern world is the learning of the process of learning, a continuing openness to experience and incorporation into oneself of the process of change.

This student has described how the structure of the task encouraged him to reflect analytically and searchingly on what he calls the 'nature of discourse' and on the way of thinking characteristic of a discipline. As a result of his reflective analysis, he developed a deeper appreciation of the value framework of the discipline he was studying, and an ability to work and study more meaningfully and effectively within that framework.

Example 6.6: IPR by telephone prompts analytical reflection-on-action

(See also Example 5.9)

I live a long way from the nearest Open University Study Centre. I'm not on the phone; I stay in a caravan, in a field near the local pub. My only contact with my tutor, other than through the comments on my assignments, comes when I use the pub telephone to allow me to join in an audio-conference call, with my tutor and five or six other students.

Once, last year, I was asked if I would take part in an experiment with my tutor. She told me that someone would phone me, after a conference call, and play a bit of it back to me, and ask me questions about that. I agreed – and it worked out all right, because the bar was fairly quiet that evening.

The man who phoned me had made a tape recording of the telephone conference call. He played back little snatches of it, and asked me if it reminded me what I was thinking or feeling at the time the call took place. I didn't remember many feelings. But I found that the tape recording brought back clearly some of what I had been thinking, some 30 minutes or so earlier. Whenever the tape stopped, I tried to tell the person on the phone about this. I hope I did that reasonably well. He seemed pleased enough.

When the phone call had finished, he asked me to summarize what I thought I had learned during the conference call. I could recall that there had been a few points which had been cleared up, and one or two extra ideas which I had added to my notes. But, to be honest, there wasn't much. He asked me if the call had mattered to me – and of course I said that, yes, it certainly had. He asked me why – and immediately I reminded him of the things I had been telling him about, as he had played back the recording to me.

First and foremost, it had been enormously important to me to realize that the bits I found difficult were proving difficult for the other people in the group as well. Before the conference call started, I had that sinking feeling, which I have so often. I was sure that I was the only person who was being stupid, or the only one who hadn't worked hard enough, or the only one who didn't really have the brains to pass this particular course. As the call went on, I realized that we were all in the same boat. That made a tremendous difference to me. I stopped feeling so worried about how I was getting on in my studies. That made me feel better about pressing on with my reading in this block of the course.

The other thing which came across in the call was an explanation of how well I needed to understand the material in the units, and what I needed to do to show that understanding. I hadn't really been clear about that as I studied the unit – which was probably part of the reason why I was worried.

It's interesting, you know. As a result of talking to that man on the phone, I came to see more clearly why these conference calls matter to me. So, next time we have one, I think I'll be listening to the discussion with my ear more firmly tuned in to what it is that I want from the call. And I'll feel OK next time about wondering how the others in the group are getting on, instead of hoping that the agenda chosen by the tutor will help me with my own difficulties. After all, the conference call isn't the best way to clear up my individual difficulties. The best way to do that is by an individual call from me to her, or by writing her a wee note. Anyway, when she was replying to individual difficulties, and even when it was mine that I had mentioned, I was really listening to find out how the others were reacting to this, more than to her assistance to another student or to me.

We have met here another student who is concerned about the standard of his performance, and about identifying a value framework in the subject which he is studying. Interestingly, as a result of participating in what was actually a research enquiry on behalf of the tutor, he became more aware of his learning and of how to improve it. The structure of the activity prompted his analysis of the usefulness of the audio conference tutorial to him, and of what he should seek out in the next one. Hence he was more likely – as a result of that analysis – to profit from conference calls in the future.

This example again raises the issue of the responsibility of the learner for part of the teaching and learning relationship. It also highlights the possibility that a learner's reflective and analytical awareness of what is happening in a learning process will lead to a more effective process, and to a more successful outcome, for that learner.

Other examples

Examples 5.6, 5.7 and 5.8, with which you will already be familiar, involved analytical reflection; Examples 5.3 and 5.4 were predominantly analytical, I feel, although they involved some evaluation as well. You may find it useful to revisit these examples, just to check my classification of them, and to consolidate your understanding of the type of reflection I am calling analytical. In contrast, all of the examples which you will encounter in the next chapter are non-examples of reflection which is purely or mainly analytical, since they depend entirely on evaluative reflection.

Generalization

I take analysis to be a cognitive process in which we find it useful to look for patterns and generalities, and for noteworthy exceptions – as the students in the examples in this chapter have done. We have visited six examples here, in each of which students reflected on one or more particular experiences. Through such analysis, as a bridge between the particular of an experience and a generalization, they came to an understanding, in generic or transferable terms, of what they could learn from these experiences and from their analyses of them. In some cases it was the environment which prompted or encouraged that reflection, as in the Alverno example. In others, such as the Kelly enquiry or the review of the learning journal, I suggest that it was the task itself which acted as the catalyst for moving learning and learners through analytical reflection into generalization.

I find little or nothing in these examples to suggest (for the meantime) that Kolbian reflection is, or should be, other than analytical. Do you? Please give a little thought to that question, before embarking on Chapter 7.

Before you test this, some second thoughts from me

This time I have only one theme for my second thoughts.

If it is indeed an analytical reflection which takes the learner from particular examples or experiences to the generalization of understanding and competence, must and should there not be a comparable (and reverse) process? Would this be the thinking which takes the learner back from the general into the application and testing of that in the next particular examples, thus widening the learning in new situations? That process seems distinctly neglected in my present formulation and presentation of this model by Kolb, and in the examples I am presenting of teaching which follows the Kolb cycle.

What does this process of testing entail anyway? Can we conceive it as the reverse of reflection, moving from the general to the particular instead of from the particular to the general? And why, other than in the elegant Example 5.6, is it apparently neglected in both practice and pedagogy? If it has as much potential to expedite progress around the cycle as does reflection, is the Kolbian approach not seriously incomplete until this, too, is equally developed and understood?

Should we not consider and plan just as deeply for the testing process which takes us from a newly formed generalization to the next experience, as for reflection? Would this be a form of activity derived from the thinking of Popper, encouraging the somewhat negative search for counter-examples and disproof? Or should it be a different type of testing, positively seeking confirmation and refinement?

Dear John

I think I've got the hang of your argument that the bridge from experience to generalization is mainly analytical – provided you agree to include the word 'mainly'!

But if that's the case, I can't for the life of me see where evaluative reflection fits in. I regard analysis as being mainly concerned with dissecting and maybe rearranging things, to lead to deeper or fuller understanding. Evaluation, on the other hand, is about making a judgement about understanding or performance. As a result, I see the evaluation process as quite different from analysis, in method and outcome. So would analytical and evaluative reflections not be equally different – in form and in purpose?

What is involved in evaluative reflection, anyway?

7

What is Involved in Evaluative Reflection?

Introduction

Before we get on to the purpose of this chapter – and that of Chapter 10 – I feel it will be helpful to make sure that you and I are using certain familiar words with the same meaning. So I'll devote a few paragraphs to tidying that up, or attempting to do so. I then have fewer examples than usual, for a reason which I will explain before I present what I have. Similarly I'm somewhat short on further examples and even non-examples. To compensate, however, there's quite a lot to think about under the headings of generalizations and second thoughts.

Vocabulary

I see evaluation as a process which leads to the making of a judgement in relation to a set of values or criteria; and one in which the judgement possibly leads to a decision. When I go out for a meal, I evaluate the items on the menu and make a judgement about which is most attractive to me for the main course, according to the criteria for selection which matter to me on that particular evening. When the chosen dish has arrived and I have consumed it, I may evaluate what I was given, and decide if I made a good choice. In much the same way, when I study a course as a student, I may evaluate in advance the usefulness of the texts which are rec-ommended – and decide which I will use most heavily in my studies. Or when I write an assignment in draft, I may evaluate my hard copy of that, identify where it falls short of my aspirations, and decide what to do about these discerned weaknesses.

The evaluative judgement which I make may take the form of a qualitative grade, or a mark, or a decision on a binary scale such as pass/fail. We tend to describe this special case of evaluation as assessment. An undergraduate examin-ation which yields a marks list is such an assessment; and assignments are assessed if they are given a mark (78 per cent) or a grade (B+). Equally, the quality of research in an academic department is assessed when it is rated 4 or 5 on a nationally recognized five-point scale; and in the recent past the teaching in a department was assessed when it was judged 'Highly satisfactory' by the Scottish Higher Education Funding Council.

The distinguishing feature of assessment, as I use that word here, is that a person or a person's work (or a Unit or its work) is evaluated in such a way that one of the outcomes is a mark or grade or rating, on some known scale which can be either norm-referenced or criterion-referenced. In norm-referencing, that which is assessed is judged against the performance of other similar people or items in the same group. The recipient of an Olympic gold medal gains a norm-referenced award, just as the person who is selected by an interview panel to be offered a particular post would emerge as 'preferred candidate' as a result of norm-referenced assessment. However, candidates who, in the process of interview, are deemed to be 'not appointable' will have failed a criterion-referenced assessment; and those who pass the British driving test will have satisfied a requirement which is criterion-referenced. A criterion-referenced judgement is made by comparing a particular performance with chosen and objective criteria, and not with other performances in the same category.

The outcomes of evaluation need not be as specific as the grades or marks or even pass decisions which are called for from assessments. The evaluation process, which includes assessment as a particular case, requires that there is or should be a fairly clear mutual understanding of that which is deemed of value, and that which is not. But an evaluation does not always result in an outcome judgement which can be described on a scale or profile of judgements, as would be a feature of those evaluations which are also assessments. A column from a music critic, describing a concert which excited and disappointed in parts, would be one such evaluation.

There is a further complication, in that both assessment and evaluation may have two purposes, and hence may take two forms. An assessment may qualify or recognize the assessed person in some way, as the driving test entitles the recipient to gain a full driving licence, and as a first class honours degree entitles someone to be considered for post-graduate research work. In that case it is usually described as a summative assessment. It sums up where that individual has got to, in respect of the assessed learning or ability. Alternatively, an assessment such as is given for an assignment – even although it is expressed as a mark or grade, and contributes to the final grading of the student – should be primarily regarded as an important part of the educational process, since it is intended to help the learner to identify the current standard of their work, and/or to identify need and potential for improvement. In that case the assessment is usually described as formative. It sets out to assist in the formation of something which will meet up to the desired values or criteria. It helps to form, reform or inform improvement. But we need to beware of so-called 'formative assessments', for this has become a somewhat slippery concept. Too often the arrangement reduces to a multiple set of summative assessments, described as if their main function was feedback, but with a considerable direct influence on the final outcome. In that case they are really components of a sub-divided scheme for summative assessment.

Evaluation may also be either formative or summative. When I first prepared learning resource materials for open learning, I offered them to students as an 'extra' – on the understanding that the students in return would offer me an informed judgement on the usefulness of my materials, so that I could improve them if necessary and then decide whether or not to incorporate them in the formal programme of my department. That was a formative evaluation; for its primary purpose was to identify the need and potential for improvement. In one such case, as I laboured hard and long to devise a more effective way to teach a particularly awkward topic, I began by subjecting my materials to this type of formative evaluation, so that I could refine and improve them iteratively. Then I carried out comparative experiments, using pre-tests and post-tests with matched groups of students, to find out if my alternative approach was indeed more effective than the status quo. That was a summative evaluation of the learning from each approach. It yielded information, in the form of values for the learning gain and its significance, which enabled me by comparison to make an objective judgement about the usefulness of my alternative approach.

One style of educational evaluation which I find methodologically attractive is the process described as 'illuminative' (Parlett and Hamilton, 1972). It seeks to illuminate the situation which is described, for those who read or hear the evaluation. This is an anthropological model, in which the evaluators – as a result of their enquiries – are able to present a thought-provoking but descriptive account of process and outcomes. They do not explicitly judge or assess, although some value framework, even if covert, will undoubtedly influence the observations which they choose to make, record and present. Nevertheless, they restrict themselves to assembling and analysing data – and then report to others, whose task it is to make the evaluation of what that data tells them.

In a Third World country, I once carried out an illuminative evaluation of a laboratory programme which caused some concern for the professor in charge. When I went to the lab, I found graduate teaching assistants from an ethnic majority who were teaching students in classes which included many from an ethnic minority, who were treated with what I can only describe as calculated brutality – according to the values which matter to me. These minority students, whose command of English was pathetically poor, were judged stupid when they did not understand the instructions given to them in English. They were abused verbally, and often hit with sticks and rods, which drew blood. They learned by trial, error and punishment what not to do with the equipment before them, and naturally progressed slowly and ineffectively. The same style of teaching, with less punishment, was applied if necessary (which was seldom) to the students from the ethnic majority. The suicide rate among the ethnic minority students was alarmingly high.

When I described what I had seen, in an illuminative evaluation presented to the professor and his ethnic majority colleagues, they seemed to swell with pride. 'That's the way these damned —s should be treated', one declared – literally. I asked them to tell me what the 'good' students, from their ethnic majority, were learning, in contrast to these allegedly stupid ones. They told me, and I noted down their claim. I devised a simple way of checking the learning and progress of the ethnic majority students, without intrusive testing. I reported the (predictably) depressing findings of that in my next meeting with the staff. The lecturers now had to confront the evidence of ineffective teaching and learning, admittedly gathered and selected by me, with what they had said they did and did not value, and had felt they were achieving. My results showed beyond question (and believe me, they tried to question) that all was not as they believed and as they wished. They now sought my advice and assistance to improve the teaching and learning situation – which improvements, I may say, benefited both those from the majority and from the minority. That had been an illuminative evaluation, with a formative intent.

Thus can illuminative evaluations, in particular, inform and influence. They depend on leaving listeners and readers to formulate their own judgements, and to respond by making their own decisions for action, in the context of their own value frameworks and judgements. For that reason they are often more effective than evaluations where it is the evaluator who decides what is right and what is wrong and where changes should be made. Many of the assessments described in this chapter illuminated for students the progress of their learning, but left them to decide how they felt about that – as did the experience I described in Example 5.1, which illuminated for the students their lack of ability to describe apparatus.

One last distinction is important in the context of this chapter. It relates almost exclusively to assessment, and to the choice of the person who formulates the judgement. In the traditional British setting, the mark or grade for an examination or an assignment is usually decided by one or more academics, and is ratified by an examination board. However, in recent years it has increasingly become the practice to involve learners in the process of assessment. In peer-assessment, it is the peer group of fellow students which decides the mark or grade to be awarded to each student, individually. In self-assessment, it is the student herself or himself who determines the mark or grade, whether or not that is taken into account when the institutional examination boards reach their decisions about awards.

Notice, however, that we often use both terms, evaluation and assessment, without adjectival qualification. Since the majority of assessments are summative, we assume that to be so unless the term is qualified by the prefix 'formative'. And since most evaluations are formative, or are at least delivered in circumstances where the recipients hope to be permitted to respond constructively to any criticisms or weaknesses, we take evaluations to be formative unless specifically described as summative. That is normal usage at the time of writing.

An interim reflection on my text

In Chapter 4, I presented models which described two rather different forms of reflection. One was in the cycle attributed to Kolb, which has reflection as a stage in a progression which takes learners from particular experiences to generalizations which are applicable in a wider context. The other, in the Cowan diagram, is built on the distinctions advanced by Schön; it portrayed reflection as a standing back from the action, for a short or longer time, to take a detached view of what had been, is, or may be happening.

At the time we met these models, I mentioned the thought that some of the loops of detached reflection in the Cowan diagram were mainly evaluative. At this stage, it is as well to remind ourselves of that distinction between models, as well as between evaluative and analytical; because, as you will have noticed, I have presented many examples since Chapter 4 in which the Kolb cycle, explicitly or implicitly, has underlain the design of the structure for learning. But I have mentioned little since Chapter 4 of my own model.

That imbalance I now propose to redress, since my experience in higher education has been such that I judge the introduction of self-assessment, compatible with the Cowan model, as the most powerful factor for change and development that I have yet encountered. But I have two problems in presenting that suggestion to you. The first is that I know that self-assessment is a hobby-horse of mine, and I am reluctant to overstress it. The second and more important is that I am convinced that this feature can transform learning; but I don't yet feel able to explain confidently why and how it does that. Perhaps you will be able to help me with finding an answer to these questions, after you have considered my second thoughts.

Example 7.1: Learners reflect first on how, and then on how well

I will here describe, very briefly and only in general terms, a sequence of events which I have observed taking place in various settings, including Edinburgh and Esbjerg, Aberdeen and Aalborg, Scotland and Schleswig-Holstein.

For one reason or another, I have asked students (or teachers) to reflect (analytically) on what they have been doing and how they do it. I facilitate, but do not direct, their attempts to produce a coherent and accurate summary of that, probably on flipchart sheets. Then I ask them to describe to me, in relation to the process which they have painstakingly summarized, the difference between doing that in a satisfactory way, and doing it well. Whatever the language and the ability under scrutiny, this further task has pushed the process analysts back to the flipchart sheets, whose descriptions they have found they must expand and make more specific, before they can draw the distinctions I seek.

I conclude from these observations that engagement with the process of evaluation, which must establish criteria for performance at various levels, requires learners in addition to think more precisely or more deeply about what the process to be evaluated entails.

Example 7.2: Students reflect on how well they should be, and are, learning

During the early part of 1983, I received an Education for Capability Award from the Royal Society of Arts (RSA). This was for a first year course in which individual students had chosen their own individual syllabuses, as they studied the Properties and Use of Materials (Cowan, 1977). In the midst of the departmental celebrations which ensued, I talked to some students who had not been involved in the pilot scheme, and who were now about to pass on from their second year to the third year, where I would be teaching them design. One of them asked me why I didn't now offer a similar open learning option in respect of design. That seemed to me a useful suggestion, and one which I immediately began to negotiate with an enthusiastic group of volunteers, who were prepared to take part in a pilot with me.

The original innovation, which had really begun some eight years earlier, owed much of its inspiration to Carl Rogers' popular book, *Freedom to Learn* (Rogers, 1969). So I thought it appropriate to return to this text, before I fleshed out the details of my new student-directed design course. As it happened, I had given away my most recent and much-thumbed copy to an enthusiast whom I had met while on a staff development visit to the Middle East. I had replaced this with what I thought was the up-to-date edition – but one which turned out to be virtually a new text, as befitted the new title *Freedom to Learn for the 80's* (Rogers, 1983). In the original book, Rogers had written about what he hoped and believed could be achieved by schemes which offered autonomous and student-centred learning. In this new version, I was to find that he had written with informed hindsight – informed by many reports from his readers and disciples, so that he now felt able to describe what he knew could certainly be done. That confidence influenced me in turn to rethink the provisional commitment I had made to my pilot group.

In our negotiations, my students had been clear that they were keen to take responsibility for their learning objectives, for the methods by which they would achieve their objectives, and for the pace of their studies. But they still wanted me to undertake the assessment. I had agreed – but while I was reading this new book by Rogers, my conscience began to nag me. In less than 24 months' time, I told myself, these students would be engaged in professional work and, to a great extent, would be responsible for their ongoing professional development. This would mean that, if they were to continue to develop, they would have to formatively assess their capabilities, their needs and their achievements. But was it right, I wondered, that the development of the critical ability to be self-assessing people should be postponed until after these students had graduated? I couldn't believe that the Rogers of the second text would endorse such continuing paternalism on my part. So I decided that it was not acceptable to offer open learning at third year level with this constraint. I went back to my dozen volunteers and declined to accept responsibility for their assessment. This was a unilateral decision which they eventually accepted, though with considerable reservations. (One of my Swedish colleagues once pointed out to me that the most authoritative thing a teacher can do is to pass authority to the student!)

Our final agreement, for what we called 'Learning Contract Design' (Cowan, 1988), was a relatively straightforward one. Each week, each student would prepare on a summary sheet a list of personal learning objectives for that week. These should relate to their studies in the field of design – but it was understood between us that the students would have freedom to interpret that descriptive title across a wide range of possibilities. On the same summary sheet, each learner would outline the methods which she or he proposed to use to achieve their objectives and methods. Each student was to ask a fellow to comment on their objectives and plan, choosing someone to do that who had not provided such a commentary in the previous weeks. The learner was committed to consider the comments carefully, but was not obliged to agree with them, or even to satisfy their author if the learner disagreed and proposed to disregard the comments. The objectives and methods, and the comments together with the learner's responses, were to be posted on a noticeboard which was open to inspection by all.

The time allocated to design was about a quarter of the working week; this was now entirely at the learner's disposal. It was agreed that I would facilitate development if so required; but that I would not instruct, direct or guide, even if asked to do so. In the context of a particular request for assistance, I would at the most outline several competitive and optional learning processes which offered the possibility of being effective – thus leaving it to the learners to choose between, or to adapt or reject, my suggestions.

At the end of the week, each learner was contracted to produce something which demonstrated what had been learned, the extent to which the learning objectives had been achieved, and the learner's assessment of that progress against the declared objectives. The tangible outcomes and the assessment of them, briefly summarized on the same sheet, were now shown to a second commenting student, who provided feedback on the outcome and on the assessment of them, as they felt appropriate. This summary was also posted on the (semi-public) noticeboard. The learner, again, was contracted to consider but not necessarily to accept or respond in person to the peer judgement.

At the end of each term, the students individually assessed their work by:

- summarizing the standards and criteria which they had been striving to achieve;
- describing their performance in comparable terms;
- reporting the process of judgement by which they compared their performance with their criteria and standards.

Their mark, which was the outcome of their personal judgement, came to me in a sealed envelope, because it was a separate matter. This mark went straight into the departmental records – provided these three conditions for the process of assessment, which we had defined and agreed in advance, had been satisfied.

(All of this took place in a vocational course where a professional body accredited the degree. Obviously, I had to go to considerable lengths to anticipate the inevitable criticisms by incredulous visiting moderators, and to provide them with evaluative information sufficient to satisfy them that our standards were indeed adequate, and were rigorously maintained. How I did that is a different story which would contribute little, if anything, to the answer which I now offer to the question at the head of this chapter – although it confirms that Machiavelli has much to offer those who engage in educational innovation, and need to ward off their critics.)

The pilot I have described was, for its time, both innovative and unusual. It excited considerable interest, from an assortment of educational visitors whose questioning and comments were in accordance with their academic reputations. As a result, some of the students were prompted to reflect deeply and extensively on their year-long experience, particularly after it had concluded. Three of them even opted to prepare a paper (Boyd *et al.*, 1984) on the subject, and presented it to a conference on the Development of Professional Competence run by the Society for Research into Higher Education. The response which I wrote to that paper by invitation some months later was published together with it by the Royal Society of Arts in the same occasional paper (Cowan, 1984b).

I hope it will be acceptable to the students, and to you, if I summarize in my own words what they extracted from their experience. Some of the students were encountering truly open learning for the first time; but some of the pilot scheme students had, two years earlier, taken the Alternative Syllabus course (actually the 'Course without a Syllabus') which had gained the RSA award (Cowan, 1980b). This subset of the group were now able to compare open learning which featured self-assessment to criteria selected by the learners, with open learning which had been teacher-assessed and was criterion-referenced. The student paper and review were prepared by three members of the latter subset, who perceived self-assessment to have had a significant formative impact on their (open) learning. They felt able to make justifiable comparisons, describing changes in what they had concentrated on in their learning (the actual syllabus), changes in how they had studied (the depth of their learning), and in how they had tried to develop personally.

I will first summarize their accounts of the learning outcomes. I draw on a visit to the Civil Engineering Learning Unit by David Boud, who is an authority in the field of self-assessment (Boud, 1995). He cross-examined some of the pilot scheme students after it was all over, and when they had just entered the final (fourth) year of their studies. They had now rejoined the students who had been taught design conventionally. All had just been engaged in a two-week design project, wherein the members of the experimental group (like their teachers) had encountered startling differences between the students from the pilot study group and those who had been conventionally taught.

A student from the pilot group told Boud:

> *They* had been taught so much in their lecture classes, about all sorts of detailed aspects of design. They all had piles of notes that would have choked a horse. *We* had very little, and we were conscious that there were many of the topics which *they* had studied, which *we* hadn't covered at all. But *they* had forgotten most of it – and when they went back to their notes, they found it difficult to make sense of them. On the other hand, *we* had learned how to learn and how to use people and read to good effect in books and journals. *We* knew how to find what we wanted, and we had developed the ability to understand things on our own, even if we had never encountered them before. And we had effective techniques for revising, and for everything else that was asked of us.

Boud asked this student about the traditional fourth year lecture classes which the students had attended, and was told of the differences they had found in that situation, as well:

> I used to make notes of what the lecturers wrote on the board, or showed us on the overhead projector, or – if there was nothing written down – of what they

said. I don't do that any more. I listen carefully to what they are actually speaking about, and I make notes of what they are really trying to say, which is often hidden away inside all of that.

The students in the self-assessing group devoted care, thought and purposeful-ness to considering what would matter to them in their learning and development, and to pursuing that – above all else. Rather like the Alverno students in Example 6.3, they set process on a par with content in their integrated goals for undergraduate learning and development. They decided again and again that they needed to concentrate on how to do things. And, because they did that, and because they were themselves frequently assessing their progress towards such (process) goals, they were constantly thinking about how well they were doing whatever it was, and constructively and effectively considering how they might do it better.

Boyd (Boyd and Cowan, 1986) summed up all of this by saying that being involved with the formulation and setting of criteria gave her ownership and intim-ate understanding of her goals, which meant that her learning and development were always purposefully directed towards them. She also maintained that she had to identify the detail of her performance, so that she could compare it with her goals and standards, and make the judgements of her self-assessments. In consequence, she became, in effect, an active manager of her own learning and development – seeing at the time what needed to be done, and acting accordingly. Her learning profited in consequence, she maintained, since she was confident that she knew herself and her thinking better than anyone else could ever do.

I submit that this pilot (Cowan, 1988) was a year-long experience in which reflec-tion-in-action was predominant. The end-of-term self-assessments, and one or two crisis sessions in mid-term, occasioned reflection-on-action. The end-of-term assessments, as they were completed, became reflection-for-action, leading to marked changes in aspirations, methods and work styles in the following term. Although the individual activities of the learner-directed programme depended on Kolbian (analytical) reflection, the driving force which made this experiment such a success was Schönian (evaluative) reflection.

Example 7.3: Students reflect on the making of judgements about their learning

The Open University course D300: *Professional Judgment [sic] and Decision Making* lays considerable emphasis on the making of professional judgements, and on the unsound outcomes which can often emerge. I must declare my view that much of the value of this splendid course lies in the depth of the reading which must be stud-ied, particularly in the medical and paramedical professions, but also from assorted sources on judgemental topics, and in the application of these concepts and meth-ods in difficult contexts. However, the development of a D300 student's ability to make judgements probably takes place most significantly through self-assessment, and in the formulation of student judgements associated with the submission of assignments. These are the aspects of the course which constitute this example.

Before they begin their studies, and indeed before they have read much in the course materials, D300 students are required to submit a 'Prior'. In this, they set out something of their past experiences as students. They identify (from examples which they are asked to provide) the qualities which they associate with a praiseworthy course and with a praiseworthy tutor. Their D300 tutor comments very little on this prior declaration of values and expectations, merely noting what is said there, and expressing interest in the experiences described. Tutors are aware of the danger that any comment may be taken as a judgement, or approval; they attempt to avoid that possibility as far as possible. The Prior is returned with these comments to the student, for use at the end of the course, as I will describe shortly.

Each time students submit an assignment, they have to self-assess it; they must also estimate their probabilities for the mark which will be awarded by their tutor. Note that it is not unusual for tutor and student to differ in the marks awarded. Students consequently come to discover that there are admissible and respectable differences between sound but different judgements, according to the use of different but acceptable criteria, weightings and processes – as well as different perceptions of performance. By the very nature of a course which wrestles with uncertainty, students are also expected to appreciate and anticipate that little in this world is certain, and that this is particularly so in respect of professional judgements.

Early self-assessments are usually fairly primitive and incomplete. There is a tendency for students simply to present a description of part (and perhaps not all) of what they have done, and to do so in terms which are more narrative than evaluative. The mark (from the student, for the student) similarly often merely appears on paper, without any explanation or justification being given – or, I suspect, having been considered.

After the third assignment (of eight), the tutors not only declare their mark as usual; they also reveal the way in which they reached it. Tutors are encouraged, although not actually required, to prepare both a decomposed assessment (assembled under a number of subheadings, each with a 'pocket' of marks allocated to it); and a composed assessment, assembled in a holistic way, as a single mark which describes the student's overall performance. Most tutors prefer to make the composed judgement first, and then almost to rationalize it, by going through the fine detail of the decomposed judgement. The reverse order is recommended by the Course Team Chair, and was the one which I myself eventually came to favour, when I was tutoring this course – because the two judgements were more distinct, and offered opportunity for triangulation and increased reliability.

Once the tutors have begun to reveal the making of their assessments, it becomes apparent to the students that they, too, should be providing a more detailed account of their attempts to specify levels or standards within their composed or decomposed frameworks. They also comprehend that their performance should be described in terms compatible with their criteria – because it must be related to these standards or levels, if their judgement based on that comparison is to be formulated objectively. Students do not find it easy to progress along the learning curve to this advanced stage of judgemental development. So tutors are advised to award their marks for the process of self-assessment according to the stage which has been reached in the course. The demand in respect of both self- and tutor-assessments increases as the course progresses; and that progression is made explicit to students from the outset.

At two stages in their studies, students prepare and submit their assessments of the course itself. These should cover all the components of the experience, from the materials and television programmes to the prescribed course reader, the administrative arrangements, and the tutorials and the correspondence tuition. It is here that they should refer back to their Prior, which was an early declaration of criteria and standards – which they may now wish to change, on reflection, for good reasons derived from their course experiences. Since the tutor is normally committed to declare his or her assessment of an assignment before opening the envelope containing the student's self-assessment, it has always seemed reasonable to me (as a tutor), to formulate my own assessment of my tutorial support and the correspondence tuition which I have provided, and to send that to my students at course assessment time. I suggest to them that my self-assessment of the tutoring is something which they should not open or read until after they have completed their course assessment. Interestingly, I receive little specific feedback on my assessments of my tutoring. But I receive strongly supportive comments about the value which students place on this practice of mine.

In the final course assessments, the students' self-assessments of the learning outcomes for them, and of the personal development which they perceive to have occurred for them in the course experience (again related to criteria and to the Prior), are usually encouraging – and thought-provoking. In 1995, for example, I tutored a small group of D300 students for whom self-assessment, or indeed any form of objective judgement, was (as usual) something with which they struggled and in which they produced poor outcomes – initially. By the time the course finished, more than half of them had discovered that they could carry out the process thoroughly and individually, to a commendable standard, and with a profitable effect on self-development. The 'before' and 'after' comparisons which they themselves made of their capabilities, including the ability to formulate judgements, were singularly persuasive and convincing.

For example, one student presented convincing data in her final self-assessments to show that, through being driven by self-assessment, she had studied in depth to an extent and rigour of demand which went far beyond her previous experience. In consequence, she had found that the tasks and standards expected of her appeared easier to achieve than ever before. In this, her first third level course, she gained a distinction – something that she had never been awarded in any of her previous OU studies, at whatever level.

A second student progressively immersed himself in what he described as an enthralling course experience. It literally dominated eight months of his life, in which he was employed during working hours as a hospital theatre orderly. He found that his thinking, particularly in the dialogue assignments and self-assessments of them, had a sharpness and generated constructive outcomes which surprised him, and motivated him intensely. This led him into deep supplementary and enrichment studies of his own choosing. He could point to examples to confirm these claims.

Another student found the methodology testing, demanding – and disturbing. Increasingly she decided to pursue her own goals to her own standards, which differed from the goals and value framework of the subject. Consequently, while feeling that the course might be validly criticized for that reason, she nonetheless described her working on the open-ended and self-assessed D300 assignments as her best teaching and learning experience to date, in all of her OU studies.

The last student in these examples tended to assess herself at much the same mark as that awarded by her tutor, but ultimately with rich qualitative judgements in addition. She eventually submitted self-assessments which had developed strikingly from the trivial, incomplete and subjective efforts in her early assignments. In her last assignment, she presented one or two devastatingly accurate and formative self-portrayals, in which she not only identified her outstanding weaknesses, but also discerned where there was scope for improvement and development which it lay within her power to bring about.

I concluded, from their summative assessments, that formative self-assessment had had a significant effect on the learning and performance of more than half of the sample I have described.

Comment

I, and others, have speculated about causation in regard to the origins of the changes in the learning and the learning experience for self-assessing students. We have perhaps done this vainly, and certainly with insufficient evidence, although the research evidence from Alverno (Mentkowski and Strait, 1983) on the effect of self-assessment is very persuasive.

In this debate, I suggest we should now focus in on two fairly well-authenticated convictions about self-assessment. The first is that learners who self-assess are constantly and effectively focusing their learning on what are usually objectives that would be associated with deep learning. The second is that, from their engagement with objectives and standards, self-assessing learners have a keener appreciation than otherwise of what it is that they are trying to do, of how well they are doing it, and thus of what they could do next to improve their performance; they are formatively self-monitoring their progress, in a directly constructive way, to further their learning and development. This applies both to the normal learning outcomes and to what I describe as the process abilities which underpin, or indeed constitute, the worthwhile learning and development which the students seek.

Other examples

Example 5.9, and possibly Examples 5.1 and 6.1, call for evaluative reflection, in my view.

Non-examples

You may now wish to reconsider carefully my assertion that all the examples in Chapter 6 call for analytical reflection. You may discern some dependence in addition on evaluation – in at least some of these examples. Perhaps it is best to say that the examples in Chapter 6 were predominantly analytical. After all, Bloom (Bloom *et al.*, 1956) would have us accept that one cannot be evaluative without being analytical first, so the examples in this chapter (in turn) have only been predominantly evaluative.

What generalization can you take from that?

It appears, from these examples, that evaluative reflection effectively encourages:

- a more focused learning experience;
- constant awareness of objectives and standards, which in turn leads to more purposeful pursuit of learning;
- regular self-monitoring which, through awareness of progress and lack of it, enables learners to direct their learning into activities which will bring about development and improved learning for them;
- deeper and more meaningful learning.

Before you test this, some second thoughts from me

1. The educational literature abounds with enquiries into the work of 'good' and valued university teachers. Most confirm that enthusiasm is one of the major attributes of such people – whether it is enthusiasm for their work or for their subject, or both. Now, it is probably apparent that the teachers in the examples in this and in the previous chapter were all highly enthusiastic. So you should consider what contribution that enthusiasm, rather than the introduction of reflection, made to the learning and the learning experience. Furthermore, the well-known Hawthorne effect testifies to the impact of novelty on performance in a range of settings. For all of the students in the examples, the situations described were undoubtedly novel. So what impact did that novelty have on the learning outcomes? Might enthusiasm and novelty not be the main causes of the results ascribed to self-assessment?

2. Is it necessarily unacceptable to achieve improvements in learning and in the learning experience, by teaching with enthusiasm and by introducing novelty and variety? Would you yourself welcome improvements which you might bring about in that way? (And if they occurred in the circumstances described, could you attribute them to self-assessment or reflective learning?)

3. How critical to the type of learning and teaching situations described in this chapter is the creation of conditions in which students feel it safe to take risks and to expose cherished standards and criteria, revealing judgements and self-criticisms?

4. It is clear that teachers and students feel that self-assessment or evaluation influences learning and the nature of the learning experience, to a considerable extent. But is that process reflective, in the sense that the word has been used to date in this text? And, if it is reflective, where does it relate to the Kolb cycle or any of the other models set out in Chapter 4? Is it not more an influence on the depth and intensity of the learning, rather than an influence on the learning and development itself – which still depends on analytical reflection, occurring elsewhere or at other times?

5. Should we be going even further than those who dislike being confronted with either/or decisions, and describe the role of reflection in learning in terms which allow that both analytical (Kolbian) and evaluative (Schönian) reflection can combine, as in the Cowan model? This can incorporate Kolbian spirals (Figure 4.2.2) in the surges of activity between major reflective loops which are for, in and on action; such spirals are often predominantly analytical. (Perhaps this is the most important caveat of all, in this group of second thoughts.)

6. It appears that involvement in self-assessment, even when that makes no contribution to a recorded mark or grade, may have a powerful impact on learning and on the learning experience. If so – and this remains to be confirmed – how does it happen, how can we facilitate it knowingly and most effectively, and to what extent should we be passing the responsibility for monitoring the self-assessment process, like the self-assessment itself, to the student? I have yet to find my own answers to these questions. Should that deter me, and you, from believing in the potential of self-assessment and from offering it on a pragmatic basis?

Dear John

Most of your examples come from engineering and the study skills area. So they are not much use to me, because my subject is quite different.

    I'd like you to offer me, and others who don't teach in your discipline area, something directly useful to us, please. Or do you seriously believe we can adapt something from your teaching to ours?

8

How Can You Adapt Ideas from My Teaching, for Yours?

Introduction

I'm a bit disappointed in that letter; it asks a question which is often posed, but which I had hoped this book would have answered already. I'll try to answer it briefly, and then give examples to illustrate that response. First, my answer.

The whole message of the Kolb cycle, for me, is that one way to learn is to look for patterns within families of problems or tasks, which link them together because the underlying framework is common to them all. If that is true for our students, then how much more true it should be for us, too. In this chapter, then, I propose to take some examples of teaching which we have met already in these pages, and operate on them in two steps, following the Kolb cycle, of course. First of all, I'll try to extract the underlying framework, as I've called it – which will be a Kolbian generalization. Then I'll test it out as a generalization, by checking if it can apply in two other different disciplines and situations.

Let me put that another way. I often find myself asked for suggestions, by a teacher who has to deal with the design of a teaching and learning difficulty, in a specific situation with particular features. When I respond with an acceptable solution, I am given credit for being creative. But I'm usually only applying a familiar framework, clad with new details appropriate to the new situation. If there are only seven original jokes, I suspect there are not many more original frameworks for learning activity. Frameworks for teaching and learning are, or should be, interdisciplinary. So there aren't too many different schemes, and we don't really need too many – because we have so much we can utilize again and again, taking the same framework and just giving it different cladding.

To illustrate that point, I will not work here with any of the examples which would make my task easier. The Dumfries study skills story (Example 2.1), for example, is already interdisciplinary, since it brought together students from a variety of faculties and courses. And the Interdisciplinary Studies course, (Example 2.3), although it only involved students of civil engineering, had widespread interdisciplinary aims. These present insufficient challenge in the present context, where I seek to show that ideas about how to teach can transfer readily from one discipline to another.

So let's test this assertion of mine by starting with the example which so often turns off listeners or readers who claim that they don't understand anything about engineering. I'll try to identify and transfer the framework in Example 2.2 which concerned the use of worksheets on the overhead projector, while teaching applied mechanics. And then I'll move it about as far away from technology as we can go.

Example 8.1: Transforming Example 2.2

The experience

I hope you'll remember that this was the example in which I gave my students worksheets which contained a number of problems, all in the same 'family'. And then I took one of the students, almost blindfold, through the method I had in mind for dealing with any problem on the sheet, so that the student could obtain the desired answer whatever example he or she had chosen. All of the examples were mathematical in nature, of course.

My generalization

You should compare my framework with the original and full description in the example, to check that I am playing fair at this stage. Here, then, is my abstraction:

1. *Assemble a family of examples* which can all be tackled by the same method.
2. Let a student *choose one example*, without telling you which one it is.
3. Take the student through that example, by *spelling out what to do*, but without reference to the particular example on which the student is working.
4. *Show the class the method* you have been following.
5. Give them, in groups, another worksheet, with *another similar family of tasks* which they should be able to carry out.
6. Arrange for each student to *tackle a different one of these tasks*.
7. Ask groups to consult and prepare a sheet of *generally applicable instructions*, like those you used in your demonstration, for the new family.
8. Get them to *test it out* on another example chosen by a student from another group.

Testing that out

In a classics course dealing with fifth-century (BC) Athens, students may have encountered the classification of Greek vases – according to a methodology which we need not detail here. Similarly the students may have learned to classify Greek swords and shields.

Again, let's apply the generalized model and see what we come up with. I'll leave it to you to keep an eye on the steps in the original, and make sure that I'm not over-simplifying. Here's my advice to a classical colleague about what she might do:

1. *Assemble a family of examples* of vases which can all be classified by the same method.
2. Let a student *choose one vase*, without telling you which one it is.
3. Take the student through that example, by *spelling out what to do*, but without reference to the particular example on which the student is working.
4. *Show the class the method* you have been following.
5. Give them, in groups, another worksheet, with *another similar family of tasks* – this time relating to the classification of shields – which they should be able to carry out.
6. Arrange for each student to *classify a different one of these shields*.
7. Ask groups to consult and prepare a sheet of *generally applicable instructions*, like those you used in your demonstration, for this new family.
8. Get them to *test it out* on an example of another shield, chosen from the sheet by a student from another group.

Testing it out again

In the Open University course *Professional Judgment and Decision Making* on which I taught, students with a strong background in social sciences study can have difficulties with the numerical part of the syllabus. For example, they may struggle to construct decision trees, and to find values for them, and then to use these values to reach decisions. The descriptions of the situations for which a tree may be desired can be complex, and thus make it challenging to extract the vital information from among the particular detail. When I was tutoring this subject, I decided to borrow the framework I had used with my first year civil engineering students. I couldn't give all the information about a family of individual problems on one acetate for an overhead projector, so I prepared a folder of descriptions of situations where decisions have to be made.

I linked this to another numerical topic which also created problems for many students with a social science background – which was the virtually predetermined sequence of calculations to determine the predictive value of a positive test result in a diagnostic medical test! Many students on this course find even that vocabulary and certainly the associated calculations demanding or off-putting – so much so that the course team have called this part of the syllabus 'the hard stuff'.

I transferred my civil engineering method, then. Here's what I did on this occasion:

1. I *assembled a family of examples* of decision trees which could all be tackled by the same method.
2. I let a student *choose one example*, without telling me which one it was.

3. I took the student through that example, by *spelling out what to do*, but without reference to the particular example on which the student was working.
4. *I showed the class the method* I had been following.
5. I gave them, in groups, another worksheet, with *a family of tasks* which involved calculating the predictive value of a positive test result – tasks which they should have been able to carry out.
6. I arranged for each student to *tackle one of these tasks*.
7. I asked groups to consult and prepare a sheet of *generally applicable instructions*, like those I used in my first demonstration, for the new 'family'.
8. I got them to *test it out* on another example, chosen by a student from another group.

In the end, having provided this activity as a revision exercise following a diagnostic pre-test which confirmed the students' declared needs, the post-test (also diagnostic) confirmed substantial progress had been made.

Verdict

The judgement should be yours, and not mine. Try to relate this framework to a familiar and common task in your own discipline. Did that first example yield a generalization of a teaching method which would transfer to your (different) discipline and situation?

Example 8.2: Transforming Example 5.2

I choose now the example of dialogue assignment writing, which is an example which I suggest many would regard as typical of the soft subjects, like social science or humanities. I choose to attempt a transfer through generalization into a demandingly hard subject area, like engineering.

The experience

This example concerns a situation in which the course team values questioning. The dialogue form chosen for the course units, the video-tapes and the assignments witnesses to that. There is never a commitment to a 'correct' answer. The materials value questioning more than answering.

That is why the course materials, which I did not describe in the earlier account of this innovation, were presented as a dialogue in which the course team chair and a guest authority argued out almost every point made, without necessarily reaching a conclusion, or agreeing. The underlying idea is that the sharper the questioning, the deeper the thinking – because there can be scope and encouragement for multiple interpretations. The course team, in designing an assignment strategy, had opted for a format which made it clear to the students that they were expected to question the 'wisdom' presented in the course materials, which was to be applied by them to a task set as coursework. In the original, the prompt for questioning was the dialogue format, which quickly became and felt stilted if there was not active questioning.

In the dialogue assignment, the learner came to probe her or his own arguments, as the model in the materials has exemplified. Even when the assignment was marked, the tutor asked questions rather than offering answers or judgements.

My generalization

1. The teacher declares that a course objective is to stimulate sound questioning and critical thinking.
2. The teacher chooses a task style in which sound or sharp questioning is not only expected, but valued and rewarded.
3. The teacher demonstrates what that kind of questioning might look like.
4. The student now tackles a similar task which is not straightforward, which uses the course material, which calls for thinking, which may have more than one reasonable answer, but which makes considerable use of course material.
5. The structure of the activity calls for frequent questioning by the learner of what is being said, written, thought or decided.
6. The teacher does not immediately, or even subsequently, declare a 'right' answer, although gross errors and omissions may be pointed out later.

Testing it out

In this testing, I confess that I am using developments which occurred before the dialogue assignment, and were not derived from it. I do not see that this reverse chronology invalidates my argument, though. I simply desire to demonstrate to you that a useful idea for a framework can translate into another situation and discipline – but not that one need be derived from the other, in every case.

For my first transfer example, I take an activity run in Heriot-Watt University at first year level by my colleague, Derek Fordyce. This was in a numerate subject called fluid mechanics.

1. On several occasions, within two-hour time slots, Derek reminded the class of the emphasis he had placed on the importance of asking good questions (which was not new to them) and explained how that demand would figure in assignments and examination questions, for which the activity to come was a preparation.
2. He then allocated students to groups with between four and six members. He presented a fairly demanding question which went beyond the simplification of reality which so often happens in engineering studies. He chose, for example, the flow of fluid in a non-standard pipe system. These systems had some familiar features to which the formulae and theories of the course had been applied,

but others which had not previously been considered. The class had studied flow and pressure loss in pipes, and pressure losses at bends; but not losses at T-junctions and Y-junctions. Thus the problem was not straightforward, called for thinking, and might well have had more than one reasonable answer. He gave the groups which had been set up plenty of time to formulate their solutions, having warned them of the format of what was to follow.

3. He chose one group, and asked them to come to the front and present their solution. As they did so, they were constantly questioned – at first by Derek, and even if their thinking was sound.

4. As the class began to pick up the idea of setting up a questioning culture, the questioning moved easily and naturally to the other students, with another group's solution to probe.

5. Foolish questions were challenged in turn, across the room, or even by Derek from the front.

6. In all of this, Derek volunteered no judgement whatsoever. Even in the case of a brilliantly perceptive solution, which was rare but not impossible, he would question and probe – as if unconvinced. It was left to the class to go on thinking and judging, and to reach their own conclusions – probably after they left the room.

The sharper the questioning, the deeper the thinking – because the problem allowed scope for fundamental thinking about the subtleties of fluid mechanics.

Verdict

It is a far cry from professional judgement to fluid mechanics. Perhaps for that reason the parallel between the two examples may seem too stretched for you to accept it as demonstrating the existence of a common underlying framework.

Let's try a simpler transfer, then, in which the derivative adheres more strictly to the underlying framework. It arose in a course design meeting held recently, when a module writer bewailed her difficulty in getting students to question and think about her subject matter, which happened to be scientific, but was descriptive rather than numerical or formulaic.

Testing it out again

I took my framework, and began from the format of examination or assignment questions in her existing course. This did not prompt the type of thinking the teacher wished to encourage. I suggested to her that she might:

1. declare a marking schedule in which at least half the marks for responses would be for exploring the other side of the position from that which the learner favours;

2. refrain from disturbing the establishment, and the students, by (almost) retaining the standard question form in which a statement is presented, often within quotation marks, when the student is merely told to 'Discuss'. But spell out the

demand of the question differently. Use a rubric which asks for four distinct responses, for the traditional 20 marks:

(a) *State* whether you agree or disagree with this statement.   (0)
(b) *List* the main points you would make in support of your view.   (5)
(c) *List* the main points you would expect to be made in a counter-
    argument by someone who had good reason to disagree with you.   (5)
(d) *Explain* how you would respond to these points, in order to convince
    a listener to accept the position you declared in (a).   (10)

3. provide model questions and answers of varying standards, and ask groups what marks they would give to each of the answers and why – these should be justified and explored in group discussion;
4. then use this same rubric as a format for some coursework tasks, in both forma-tive and summative continuous assessment, to familiarize students with this style of demand;
5. emphasize the demands of items (c) and (d), when marking and commenting on submitted coursework. Encourage discussion of how to meet the demands;
6. never declare or imply a 'right' answer – although she might point out gross errors and omissions, but even then would only do so some time later.

Verdict

This approach was accepted by the module writer with some enthusiasm, and fea-tures in the final scheme which she submitted.

However, in this as in other cases, the final judgement should be yours, and not hers or mine. *Did* that first example yield a framework or generalization which transferred to different disciplines and situations?

Example 8.3: Transforming Example 5.1

The experience

In this example, as I hope you may recall, I set up a situation in which students who felt they had nothing more to learn about communication, at least insofar as describing apparatus was concerned, came to a contrary conclusion within a short time.

I give descriptive titles to my underlying shapes and frameworks for activities. This framework, for reasons which may be apparent to aficionados of A.A. Milne (Milne, 1926), I have always called 'Heffalump Trap'. With that title in mind, and having given away my secret once again, let's look for the features of the framework underlying the activity I described earlier in some detail.

My generalization

I sum up the 'describing apparatus' activity in these short terms:

1. Ask the learners to declare what they have mastered, if you expect that they will claim more than is within their ability.
2. Set up a situation in which they should be able to demonstrate that competence.
3. Check performance against expected outcomes – in public.
4. Note the striking discrepancy; and confront the learners with that.
5. Invite the learners to decide what to do about it.

Testing it out

Let's explore this framework in the field of staff development, which I suppose is the discipline area of education.

1. Alan Harding and I had a somewhat wicked way of beginning a week's pro-gramme of staff and educational development with any lecturers from any single department and degree course who brought to the workshop activity a declared confidence in what they were doing, and in their competence to do it soundly. We introduced the group to the words in Bloom's taxonomy (see below) (Bloom *et al.*, 1956). Although this has been criticized, we had found that it was nonethe-less a useful framework for initial discussions of educational goals, because it uses words of whose meaning there is a common and shared agreement.
2. We divided our participants into four or more groups and asked them to decide what proportion of their teaching and learning *should* concentrate on:

   - evaluation
   - synthesis – or creative problem-solving, according to the discipline
   - analysis
   - application of understanding
   - understanding
   - knowledge.

   We required them to produce percentage figures for the subdivision of their goals under these headings, for each year of their course. They usually made powerful claims for coverage of items at the top of the scale.
3. Once the groups had each told us that they had reached agreement, we gave them prepared acetates on which they entered their figures, which they then gave us for display in plenary. We had arranged the columns on the acetates so that the results from all of the groups for, say, the final year of the course, could be displayed at one time. I cannot recall an occasion when these showed an acceptable consensus. Clearly there was disagreement here on which they, and we, needed to work.
4. As they struggled to digest that inference, we asked them in passing if they felt that the end-of-year assessments should reflect what they wanted the students to learn. This trivial question, answered affirmatively, diverted attention from their dilemma about their disagreement over goals. We then produced some of their

past examination papers, usually for the final year, which we 'just happened to have with us'. We asked them to show us, in the examination question coverage, the amount of testing of the higher level goals for which their acetates had made bold claims. There were few such examples to be found – something I have also encountered, incidentally, during Teaching Quality Assessment in some of our most highly regarded British departments.
5. We asked them what they wanted to do about it – and left them on their own, with time to come to the conclusion that they wanted our help in redesigning the curriculum.

This Heffalump Trap, like the original one, had caught people who had dug it for themselves. They were consequently more prepared to make a new beginning – provided the reception of the embarrassing message had taken place in circumstances which did not provoke an angry defensive reaction, or hurt.

Testing it out again

I'll try another switch, to technology, which I admit is not so far from the engineering with which this sequence began. But please note that, had I not told you the subject area, or had you not deduced it from my academic qualifications, this example could apply – I suggest – in virtually any discipline. Please look back again to my original generalization of the method.

1. When I contact a department for which I have recently been appointed external examiner, I often ask them to tell me about their final year project. Invariably, it sounds good – especially when I ask about the criteria against which it is judged. I ask, without making a fuss about it, if these criteria are made known to the students. And I tend to be told – with some mild surprise – that of course the criteria are tabled and explained, and naturally influence much of what the students do, during the year.
2. Later in the same conversation I suggest that, in the course of my travels and therefore at no cost to the department, I would quite like to meet with the students, after they have made a start on their projects. 'That would be grand', they say, 'We'll arrange that.' 'Perhaps I could run a short workshop, to let them work with their External?' I suggest. 'Oh, we've never had an External who did that, but it seems a good idea.' 'Would the staff be interested to join in?' I ask. 'I'm sure some at least would want to come along', they say. 'And perhaps share with me in the workshop?' I suggest gently. 'Why not?' comes the unsuspecting reply.

On the day, I gather the students in one room, and put them in groups of about six. I ask them to summarize for me on flipchart sheets what they expect me to look for when I am judging the worth of the projects which will come to me at the end of the year, and the qualities which I should notice in a very good piece of work. They work with a will to answer my question. In a separate room I take the staff, almost all of whom have come along out of curiosity, and give them the same task. In their case, I let them work in plenary, with one of their number acting as scribe.

3. I go back to the students' room, and we Blu-Tack the sheets on one wall. They are written in the students' own words, but much the same message comes from every group, although I have discouraged collaboration.
4. I then invite the staff to bring their flipchart sheet through, and display it on the opposite wall. The staff immediately go to see what the students have written, and the students flock around the staff summary. The symbolism of the use of opposite walls is apt. For both walls carry starkly different messages, which differ in much more than the choice of words.

   As tactfully as I can, I point out, with crossed arms and challenging index fingers, that the staff seem to want the students to go *that* way, while the students think that they are expected to go *this* way. I suggest that it might be an idea for the two groups to talk to each other, because if the students have got the wrong idea of what's expected of them, how can they be expected to deliver work which will be judged sound? I tell them that I had a colleague whose granny was prone to point out that 'If you don't know where you're going, any bus will do'. Staff begin to protest loudly that 'We told them'. I point out as gently as possible that the evidence on the walls suggests that, whatever message was sent and with whatever force and conviction it was told, it has not yet been heard and understood.
5. I suggest that it might be an idea for them to talk to each other. Then I depart, quietly – and await developments which seldom fail to emerge, constructively.

Verdict

I again leave the decision with you, asking if the underlying framework for these three diverse activities is indeed a common one. If so, is it one that *you* might use, whatever your discipline, should your purpose be to confront complacency?

Notice that the argument here is that frameworks can transfer acceptably and usefully between disciplines – provided the teachers concerned share commonality of purpose.

Example 8.4: Empathy and co-counselling

In this last example, I write as a teacher who has found it useful to harness the potential of detailed questioning by a peer who seeks to empathize with a learner, and who will stimulate thinking by the questions asked, and the reaction which they provoke in the learner. I'll present this last shape or framework in somewhat less detail, and leave it to you to test the underlying common ground yourself.

I think of this framework as 'Kelly', from the phrase which the psychologist George Kelly used somewhere about being able to 'get inside someone's skin and jump around like them'. I'll go straight to the generalization, which is a simple one.

Generalization

1. Arrange for a peer to listen, read, observe and/or ask questions so that they can identify with the position of the learner.
2. Expect the person seeking to develop, even without discussion, to be prompted into reflection and consequent development by this questioning, and the thinking which it provokes for them.

Testing it out

My three examples on which I invite you to test out that shape are:

- The interaction of facilitative commentator with journal writer, in Example 2.3 and others.
- The co-counselling activity when two learners reported their recorded protocols to each other, and considered what these described (Example 9.1).
- The constructive peer scrutiny of draft coursework, in which much of the learning happens before the constructive comments are reported back (Example 6.1).

Do the two steps of my generalization, and my summary of the intention, apply to each case – and offer you another shape for your repertoire? I hope they do.

Overall generalization

It will be clear that I firmly believe that the marriage of underlying principles and the desired learning objective constitutes a pedagogical shape or framework for a commendable teaching and learning situation. I argue that such a framework is independent of the discipline in which it happens to be used, since it relates only to the category of intended outcome. For that reason, I believe that such formats are usefully transferable in principle (though not in detail) by any teacher who has a similar learning goal and is prepared to exercise a little ingenuity while pillaging good ideas.

It has been, and is, for you to test out that input from me. If it proves valid, then the outcomes for you as a teacher will be rich ones. You will not need to do much of your own design of class activities but will be able to work from discernable frameworks in any subject area, to which you will simply need to add particular cladding to suit your particular situation.

Some second thoughts from me

I'm afraid I don't have any reservations to offer regarding the sincere beliefs which I have aired frankly. My sole comment is to ask if you noticed that I have not made any reference to, or use of, the Cowan diagram or Schönian reflection. You may wish to consider why that should have been so.

Dear John

I must make a start soon, and see how I can get on. But I still can't quite picture how I can move from this discursive stage, which is all on paper and in my mind, to everyday action on my part.

What can I do to make sure that I think through all the implications before I begin? How should I make sure that I'm well advised and informed? Where will I get my final plans from? These plans must above all be mine, and securely related to my subject, my situation, and my priorities for my students. But they still mustn't be amateurish; I couldn't be comfortable with that.

Give me your advice, then; pinpoint where I can get inspiration, example and support — for what may lie ahead of me. How should I get started?

9

How Should You Get Started?

A warning from the past

> There is nothing more difficult to take in hand, more perilous to conduct, than to take a lead in the introduction of a new order of things. Because the innovation has for enemies all those who have done well under the old conditions, and lukewarm defenders in those who may do well under the new.
>
> (Niccolò Machiavelli *The Prince*, Book VI)

Introduction

The pattern in this chapter is almost the same as before. I'll present four examples, and then go straight into generalizations and the usual self-discipline of second thoughts.

I'll begin with what should perhaps be given the title which one of the publisher's reviewers suggested for this volume: 'Confessions of an Educational Innovator'.

Example 9.1: The first steps for John Cowan

Please don't regard me as someone who is radically different from you, who are my readers – except in that, at the beginning, I was at a disadvantage. I could draw on fewer examples than you now have before you; and so I had to make my own mistakes from scratch. If I could make progress in these circumstances, will there not be a large part of the answer to your question in my experience – which you can follow?

I got into this business of reflection in learning almost accidentally. I felt dissatisfied with the teaching and learning situations I was creating for my students. I was sure that these students had the potential to do better than I was managing to encourage them to do, in my conventional classes. This was particularly so in respect of the development of those all-important problem-solving abilities which involve a qualitative understanding of structural behaviour. That's why I began to research the nature of my students' learning, and of their experiences in the teaching and learning situations which I created for them.

At the same time, conscious of my inadequacy, I searched in the educational literature for inspiration. I found that there were several eminent educationists writing at that time, explaining what was wrong with higher education, and the ways in which it encouraged superficial and ineffective approaches to learning (Bligh, 1971; Entwistle, 1972; Bligh *et al.*, 1975; Marton *et al.*, 1984). I found a fair amount of descriptive material about individualized learning (Postlethwait *et al.*, 1964; Keller, 1968). But I didn't find anything to show or suggest a pedagogical basis from which people like me could work to bring about improvements in our teaching.

Consequently I began, very tentatively, to imitate some studies by the educational psychologists whose work I had encountered. For I felt that I first needed to find out what was happening in terms of my students' learning, in the situations for which I was responsible and which I wanted to improve. In the beginning, I arranged for my students to talk out their thoughts aloud, as they tackled the kind of problems which I wished them to be able to solve (Cowan, 1977, 1980a).

When I looked at the end results, as they appeared in the sketches and calculations on the students' worksheets, I was almost too embarrassed to listen to the accompanying tape recordings. The students' attempts to solve my straightforward problems had produced dreadful results, which were either riddled with obvious errors or simply completely wrong. But I forced myself none the less to listen to the tapes. Immediately I felt humble. For, time after time, I found myself eavesdropping on a student problem-solver who had been making a valiant effort to apply his or her fairly sound understanding, and who had perhaps made but one mistake in the early stages. Thereafter that student had struggled commendably with the consequential complexities which their mistake had created for them. It was a little bit like reading the log of a ship's captain who had been trying to follow the sailing instructions from Plymouth to Australia, and who had mistakenly turned right at Gibraltar instead of left – but went on afterwards, zealously trying to do as he had been told.

From this research, I became aware of radical differences within the assortment of approaches to problem-solving which were followed by my students – differences which they carefully concealed in any paperwork which they produced for me and for my colleagues. It was as if their revered teacher had demonstrated in class the 'right way' to think and to solve problems, and had exemplified, on the chalkboard or on the screen, or in the textbook or handout, what the students had taken to be a model solution. Even when students thought about, and successfully solved, a problem in a radically different way from that which authority had demonstrated, they still presented their written solution in what they appeared to regard as the conventional and expected format. They concealed their 'mental problem-solving', just as people who are not numerically agile are loath to reveal their thinking when they try to carry out operations in mental arithmetic. They generated no evidence of what they had really been doing, in normal circumstances – because they hadn't seen any sign of authority offering to do that publicly, either. I asked some of my colleagues to talk out their thoughts aloud – with minimal success. But from the few offerings made available to me, I noted that experts take an almost perverse pleasure in misleadingly presenting, in public or in class, the *end* results of their thinking, with their wise decisions rationalized, and little if any revelation of their speculations, their trials – or their errors.

My studies at least began to make me aware of the nature of the wide range of learning approaches to be found within my apparently homogeneous class group. However, I soon discovered that it was a truly tedious job to transcribe the recordings (because they were seldom dictated in sentences and paragraphs, and were often of mixed quality as far as the sound was concerned). And even then, of course, I still had to analyse the transcripts, and decide how to respond constructively to them. In desperation at the magnitude of the agenda before me, and with some feelings for the tedium I was creating in the workload for my unfortunate secretary, I moved to an approach which would no doubt have horrified experimental psychologists.

I asked my student subjects to make a start (at least) on the task of analysis for me, and to summarize the processes which they had been following in the experiences for which they had recorded a running commentary. I also asked them to talk through these tentative findings of theirs, with a peer. I introduced this second stage because I sought to filter out extremes of subjectivity in the analyses by the students of their own problem-solving. In all of this, I was assisted by the fact that I had found sufficient resource to make modest payments to these students. Consequently, they felt that they were not being inspected or investigated, but were collaborating with me on a research enquiry. It was possibly for this reason that they were more willing to talk freely, when they reported their analyses to each other.

I vividly recall one of the earliest of such dialogues. One of a pair of students who had lived in the same flat since they came to university, turned in indignation to his fellow in the midst of his report on how he had tackled a particular problem, and interrupted to protest loudly: 'Three years we've been living and working together – and you've had a better way of doing that, and you never told me!'

This type of experience made me begin to ruminate about possible ways in which I might eventually persuade the students in the class as a whole, rather than in a small research sample, to identify how they tackled certain types of problem – and to make that information available to their fellows. I hoped that they might come to do this with a sophistication far beyond the type of algorithm described in Example 2.2. Hence they might come to exchange and adopt rigorous methodologies and refined personal practices which could offer individuals considerable scope for improvement. As I explored group activities to facilitate and encourage such possibilities, I found that my students were increasingly taking charge of their self-development for me – and for themselves, of course – as they became action-researchers of their own problem-solving. I also noticed that, in courses which I did not teach, these analytical and self-researching subjects of mine began to move up the class in ranking order. Self-aware students appeared to succeed – and to improve.

I read books which described, across a variety of disciplines, ways in which other university teachers were working to develop what at that time was termed

'Capability', mainly in relation to the Nuffield project on Independence in Learning, and (later) the Education for Capability campaign. I relied considerably on a few selected texts – such as Rogers' *Freedom to Learn* (Rogers, 1969) and *On Becoming a Person* (Rogers, 1961); and I drew on an assortment of accounts from innovative teachers who had tried, over the years, to develop that creative ability which is possessed by those whom engineers call designers. To be frank, I pillaged as widely and as usefully as I could, from accounts of what others were doing.

I also involved my students in the planning and evaluation of what we were doing, and in suggesting how we could go on improving it. I devoted a fair amount of my effort to formative evaluation, which informed me about how and where to improve the nature of the learning experience for my students, in these new formats which I was using. All of this contributed to our progress together. Eventually I felt able to publish one or two anecdotal accounts of what I was doing. I wrote papers and gave seminars and workshops. As a result, I met kindred spirits, who volunteered their own ideas and experiences.

And I was lucky – but perhaps that was partly because I made my own luck. Some educationists, like Graham Gibbs (Gibbs, 1987), are great believers in serendipity – but I believe it can be helped along, and I do what I can to help it. For instance, I can't recall where I had first encountered the basic idea of a reflective learning journal, as distinct from a learning diary. But I know that I had deliberately stored in my subconscious the vague notion of using – sometime – this good idea, which I had learned about in some chance encounter. I was determined to see what it held for me. So I kept it there, away in the depths of my memory from which it emerged apparently serendipitously when Derek Fordyce and I were conceiving an IDS course from scratch, and desperately seeking inspiration – borrowed inspiration, as it happened, in the case of the reflective journal. We had to conceive all the detail ourselves, of course. I know that it was about a year and a half after I had begun to require my students to keep learning journals that I encountered *The New Diary* by Tristine Rainier (Rainier, 1980), which I then found very helpful. I wonder if it would have started me off, though. I doubt that.

I certainly wouldn't have got anywhere if I hadn't been willing to take risks and experiment – and if I hadn't been able to persuade my students to go along with me, on a small scale and with a modest hope of success. Innovation, for me, has always been a joint activity which students and I have undertaken together. I also suppose I made progress because I always had a clear idea of the type of learning outcome I was trying to achieve. The result was that most of my strivings were directed towards some goal about which I was quite clear (and was perhaps too one-track minded?). Thus my successes (and failures) in making progress towards that goal became immediately apparent to us all. I admit that I made many mistakes (Cowan, 1984c, 1989); but I also recognized and built on these mistakes, trying to reverse what hadn't worked, and getting this to give me a message about what might, or should, work. It was rather like printing from a photographic negative to obtain a positive, and thus to get to the opposite of what had failed.

There were other educationists, in Britain and elsewhere, engaged in the same kind of activity as me, around the same period in educational development. But I wasn't yet sufficiently aware of them. I didn't find ways to tap into the growing body of literature which would have given me access to their experience, their theorizing, their suggestions and above all their example. Nowadays, and sadly too late, I regret that omission deeply.

I must not give you the impression that I was alone in any of my activities. I profited from some splendid partnerships. I learned from and with Alan Harding (Cowan and Harding, 1986) that, to be effective, learning must be active and systematically facilitated. I discovered with Derek Fordyce (Fordyce and Cowan, 1985) that it is possible to get so well inside your partner's skin, and vice versa, that the pair can literally think and act as one. Anna Garry (Garry and Cowan, 1987) introduced me to the importance of feelings in the learning process, and showed me how to be more sensitive and responsive to them. These were all extremely important collaborations for me, as I developed and innovated.

I will summarize. In my developmental stage, I

- concentrated on trying to find out how my students learned;
- kept my students fully informed, and carried them with me;
- turned my students into action-researchers of their own practices;
- took risks, and experimented with different ways of teaching;
- formed constructive partnerships with kindred spirits, usually only in one such partnership at a time;
- searched for people, and ideas and textbooks, which might give me inspiration or useful ideas;
- published, spoke, earned a reputation, and made contacts in consequence.

The most important of that list for me, in relation to this business of reflection, is the passing of initiative to learners who became action-researchers of their own learning. For that is what reflection eventually implies, when the ability has been fully developed.

Example 9.2: The first steps for Bob Matthew

In the early days of the Civil Engineering Learning Unit at Heriot-Watt University (Cowan *et al.*, 1973), Bob Matthew was a student of mine. This was during the period when I was most strongly influenced by Rogers, and offering freedom of pace and freedom of approach to learning outcomes, through individualized learning resource materials and self-directed learning.

After Bob graduated, he went into professional practice, and we lost touch. He moved on to University College, Cork, to teach civil engineering there. I met up with him again, when I was visiting Cork to run a staff development workshop. Some three years later, and after he had moved to Bradford, Bob and a colleague contacted me. They told me that they had been reading my publications, were critical of the way they were teaching and the type of goals they were addressing, and wanted to come up to Edinburgh, to draw on my experience. I readily agreed, and we enjoyed a fruitful two days in what was partly discussion and partly, I am afraid, monologue on my part. They caught up with what I had been doing, why I had been doing it, and what I thought I had been achieving. At the same time, they tabled and discussed part of their thinking for their next steps, while continuing other parts of that thinking on their own.

I gave them a selection of my recent publications, which they took away with them. Bob has been kind enough to describe one of these (Cowan, 1984b) as the most inspiring piece of writing he could recommend to someone minded, but not decided, to change their ways of teaching. Be that as it may, I heard little or nothing from them over the next few years, until I began to read their publications and hear at second hand of their doings. Eventually I noted with great pleasure that the Partnerships Trust had awarded a prize to Bob and colleagues for their innovations in engineering education.

As Rogers might have said, a facilitated learner is similar to a therapist's patient, in that no progress or development is likely to ensue unless the subject generates motivation, and takes the forming of the solution into their own hands. Bob Matthew began his journey to the position he now occupies because he was motivated to teach differently and better. Then he used his contacts, and went thoughtfully and with good questions to a number of people, of whom I was only one, to draw on their experience. It is foolish to attempt to reinvent the wheel, and wasteful not to begin from what is already available. In the world of innovation, it is wise to tap several sources, to note and muse on discrepancies and omissions, and to take on board that which feels comfortable to you, rather than merely that which is recommended by one other person.

That last statement, I suggest, is the key to understanding Bob's progress. His visit to McMaster University, for example, was an important watershed for him. He had met someone at a conference who had been doing some work using enquiry-based methods. Bob managed to raise sufficient funding to go to see the work on enquiry methods, while at the same time visiting Donald Woods to learn about his work on problem-solving, and the Medical School to see their use of problem-based learning. Bob found this truly inspirational – things that he had read about were working in practice; others have also experienced the same problems – and so research ensued! Bob Matthew feels that it was the process of working with, and talking to, others in similar positions that helped him to see ways forward. He spoke to a number of other people about problem-based learning. And he selected those parts of their advice and experience which he felt would work for him, in accordance with his own skills and beliefs. Over the years, he has since developed these in his own way, through building up his own self-confidence and experience. And now, of course, he finds himself passing on his thinking to people who are following him.

Educational innovation can be an extremely lonely business for the solitary explorer. Bob has worked with several partners. He stresses that a partner will question points which you yourself haven't questioned, will see possibilities which haven't occurred to you, can take on parts of the job which you don't find attractive but which your partner does, and will above all force you – just by being there – to articulate what it is that you are trying to do, which is a powerful component of creative problem-solving. Educational development is a demanding form of creative problem-solving. A partner of your own fighting weight, or above that, will share in the planning, the hoping, the work, the disappointments and the elation, and bring out the best in you. Following Rogers' model, Bob sees a partner as someone who can act as a therapist. He is clear that just having someone to talk to, to listen to you as you sound off and as you think out loud, to act as a sounding board for your own learning (even sometimes reading a learning log), was vital for him. For most things don't work well on the first couple of iterations, and just talking it through is important.

Nevertheless, in a recent letter to me, Bob wrote:

> For me, some of my most important innovations (well, to me they are!) have been made alone. I've sought advice, discussed and so on, but at the end of the day, *I* took the risk, in partnership with my learners – the students. I have always explained to them the whys and wherefores of what I proposed to do; they need to understand why I am challenging them, and asking them to work in ways which colleagues find strange, and even ridicule and belittle on occasions. If they are on my side, I can take colleagues' sniping!
>
> At the present, I feel I have pushed educational innovation as far as I can in my department. I now spend considerable amounts of time, helping, through staff development, colleagues in other departments to take the first tentative steps in changing their teaching. What a delight to see their end of module evaluations on the innovation, when they see changes in the way their students learn.
>
> While I have made many innovations in my teaching, I am not complacent, and try to keep things up to date, and monitor what I do through peer observation, outside evaluation, structured student evaluation and so on.

Example 9.3: The first steps for Judith George

I first met Judith George in 1987, when I moved to the Open University in Scotland. At that time her educational experience was extensive, particularly with regard to student support. She was (and still is) the leading authority in the United Kingdom on the use of the telephone for the support of distance learners. She was and is also someone with a keen commitment to the development of study skills. Soon it was natural that we built on that interest which we shared, to collaborate in a variety of initiatives centred on reflective learning, in an educational partnership which was to continue fruitfully for several years.

By this stage in my own educational career, I was primarily interested in encouraging my teaching colleagues, full-time as well as part-time, to become action-researchers of their own practices, and to develop accordingly. I was therefore searching for useful tools and methods of enquiry, which I could offer to enable serving university teachers to enquire in this way without becoming professional researchers – and without their needing training, or briefing of any appreciable duration, before engaging in this action-research. Judith and I worked together on the development and use of such tools of educational enquiry, which at that time was a new interest for her.

I have often encouraged my colleagues who care about learning to find occasional opportunities, at least, to experience situations as learners, rather than as teachers. I instance to them my own rewarding trip to the University of South Carolina, where my way of finding out about the Freshman Year Experience (Agnew and Cowan, 1986) had been to become a temporary student in a first year class at that university, rather than by visiting the teachers and talking with them about what they were doing.

By 1988, I had become interested in what I was reading and hearing about Alverno College. It had naturally occurred to me that the best way to find out something useful about this radical institution would be to have a student experience there, preferably from the beginning of an academic year and lasting for a few weeks. But I knew that it wasn't possible for me to change my gender, in order to go relatively unnoticed as an elderly student at this girls' college.

I therefore suggested to Judith that she might undertake such an enquiry, as a mature female student. Together we prepared a case for this visit, which was warmly accepted by Alverno faculty. And so it was that, in the autumn of 1991, Judith went to Alverno to become a first year student for three weeks. But there was to be more to it than that. For we arranged an e-mail address for her in Milwaukee. And, each evening, after classes and when other students were socializing or catching up with their work or preparing for the next day, Judith would draw concept maps of her learning during the day, and then sit down at a terminal and compile reflective learning journal entries, together with descriptions of critical incidents. She finished each long day by e-mailing this across the Atlantic to me.

Here we exploited the six-hour time difference between Milwaukee and Edinburgh. For, if I merely came in to the Edinburgh office a little ahead of my usual time, I could take an hour or so to analyse incidents, to offer semi-Rogerian comments (as in Example 2.3), and generally attempt to be facilitative (and certainly not directive) in my responses – which I sent off to be waiting on the server in Milwaukee when Judith got up at her breakfast time, six hours behind the United Kingdom. (This, I may say, was the only respect in which I ever felt educational Milwaukee to be behind Edinburgh!)

(I well recall one learning journal record, describing a class where all had gone less well than the learners, or at least the journalling learner, might have hoped. Suddenly, in the midst of her narrative account, Judith broke off to exclaim passionately: 'Every teacher should be *made* to go back to be a student once every two years.' Immediately afterwards she calmly resumed her narrative, almost as if the outburst had never occurred.)

When she returned to the United Kingdom, Judith spent two afternoons a week – carved out from a business diary which contained much evening and weekend working – to go through the Alverno papers, the concept maps, the journals and the exchanges. She set out to digest what this had said to her. In effect, she decided to prepare herself to teach in a different way in the future from that which she had followed in the past – as a result of her recent student learning experience. One immediate outcome was to be her contribution, as a writer, to the innovatory learning guide in the Open University Course A295: *Homer, Poetry and Society* (mentioned in Example 6.5). There she provided guidance for learners who had both to design an assignment question and to determine the process which they would follow in responding to it; and who, thereafter, would assess their handling of task and process in the assignment where they made their response to their own question.

Much of the initial motivation to explore other ways of teaching, with new goals or with changed priorities and certainly with a more rigorous and fundamental educational basis, probably began for Judith George as a consequence of an every-day working relationship with me. It was a relationship in which I had set out to unearth the undoubted ability and potential of a senior colleague, through working creatively with her on a number of worthwhile projects which appealed to us both. We shared thoughts and experiences, as well as plans and reasoning. I certainly did not attempt to evangelize, nor did I need to instruct or teach. I was prepared in the beginning to prompt and to share thoughts and plans with someone who began as a kindred spirit but quickly became a valued partner.

All that has happened for her since these early years has been self-directed by Judith, and has resulted from her fashioning of carefully self-structured reflection of whose framework and outcomes I have (happily) only an incomplete impression. For, as she has grown in educational innovation, so has our educational partner-ship naturally and necessarily become less close. Her thinking and innovations have involved her with others – and often with others who have become her 'junior partners' and have learned from her, in their turn.

Example 9.4: The first steps for the Inverness Five

By 1991, I yearned to encourage some of my tutorial and counselling colleagues in the Open University to tackle with me some educational objectives relating to some rather more valuable and transferable cognitive abilities, such as those which would be of direct relevance to second-level students in their studies. For some reason which I cannot now recall, I opted to concentrate on transferable abilities for second-level studies in science. This led me into the planning of an event which, at the time, was a great disappointment to me (Cowan, 1994). Nevertheless, through what has followed, this eventually transpired to have been the springboard for a rich record of curriculum development within the subsequent five-year period.

I began from a strong, but relatively newly born and certainly untested, convic-tion about any development which sets out to enhance the student learning experi-ence. Whether such an activity is in the staff or curriculum development areas, I had come to the belief that it should if possible include in the programme some real teaching of real learners with real learning needs.

I therefore recruited four tutors and eight of their students to take part in a resi-dential event in an attractive, but remote, part of the north of Scotland. The four tutors were to be residential for the entire weekend; the students were to arrive for the Saturday only. In addition to the four tutors in residence, I planned for two enquirers who would come to offer Interpersonal Process Recall (IPR, as described in Example 5.9) to illuminate and evaluate what was happening in the tutorial exchanges between students and tutors. The enquirers' work would be focused to enable students and tutor, immediately after tutorial exchanges, to recall the nature and content as well as progress of the learning experience. I included this component in my programme to provide relevant data on which the tutors might reflect – constructively.

My first of many shocks came in the opening activity of the Friday evening. I discovered that these carefully selected, well-regarded and experienced tutors of science, who professed to have thought deeply about the transferable abilities which are at the heart of their discipline, were not able to describe their own cognitive activity in their discipline in terms of the mental skills and abilities which they used in studies in science generally, and not merely in one particular context. I described the type of ability I wanted them to identify as a 'transferable skill' – an awkward title, but one in common usage. I found that, in some cases, they could vaguely identify what might be a skill – by a title, in one word or in a phrase. But, when pressed to expand on that, they had encountered insuperable difficulty in doing so.

Predictably, their students (when they arrived on the Saturday morning) had even more acute difficulties in identifying and describing even those parts of their studies with which they wished assistance in regard to the underlying transferable skills. And naturally the tutors (who had apparently given little conscious thought hitherto in their professional lives to how they themselves had come to 'think science') had few coherent notions about how to help their students to develop abilities which they, the tutors, seemed to take for granted. Fortunately, the day at least contained one useful type of experiential learning. For the IPR reports astonished the tutors, again and again, by revealing constructively several startling and totally unexpected mismatches which the enquirers reported, in what had appeared to both to be routine, and effective, tutorial interactions. (It was one such example which was reported as Example 5.9.)

After the evening meal on the Saturday, we ran a brief but sharply focused evaluation session. The students reported that they had had a useful day, which had assisted them with their learning, and had had outcomes which they identified and reported objectively and convincingly. They departed contentedly on their homeward journeys. The tutors, the enquirers and the organizer relaxed – in preparation for what were to prove the difficult discussions of the next day. For the Sunday morning had been the time I had set aside for the staff group as a whole – to summarize, to analyse and to lay plans for their return to their normal teaching. It proved a predictably depressing session, in which neither the tutors, nor I as the organizer of the event, could identify positive outcomes nor clearly see a useful way ahead.

Two of the tutors returned to everyday life and to their established educational practices, with no further engagement in this type of activity. One tutor pursued his own questions and his own initiatives, to considerable effect, but independently. Fortunately the fourth tutor, Helen Wood, who was a scientist resident in the north of Scotland, had been worried by the questions and challenges which the weekend had raised for her. She wanted to do something purposeful and effective about them. She recruited kindred spirits, at first informally and then on a rather more definite basis. Eventually she elicited expressions of interest from four of her nearby colleagues, drawn from various science disciplines. She enlisted the assistance of the organizer of the original event (me), to facilitate the meetings of this quintet, whom I quickly named 'The Inverness Five'. From a virtual disaster, and one thoughtful survivor, a phoenix activity emerged.

During the academic year which followed, the Inverness Five tutors managed much of their own tentative development. They devoted effort to experimenting in their tutorial contacts with students. They found time to try to discover what transferable cognitive skills were being demanded of their students, and of themselves, in the second-level courses which they tutored. They met to reflect on what they were experiencing and discovering. They sought my assistance on occasions, firstly to facilitate these reflective meetings and then to suggest means of enquiry which might usefully inform their further deliberations. Above all, they embarked on, and sustained, personal explorations to try to clarify in meaningful terms just what these transferable skills in science actually entailed – and, indeed, what a transferable skill actually was, in general terms.

And so it was that, two years after the first event, we six were together able to arrange a second residential weekend in the same location – but with a different structure, after more thorough preparation, and with a clear intent. We wanted to put our tentative thinking and experimenting to the test, first in this event and then throughout the academic year to follow. Once again the programme humoured my conviction that the most meaningful staff development for people who teach should involve both teaching and learning within the activity. This meant that within our programme there were again to be learners with genuine learning needs, learners who would be experiencing teaching and learning activities with valid objectives during their time with us. These were chosen from students who would be tutored by the Five in the year ahead.

There were thus four distinct groups of people at this watershed event, all of whom came for different purposes. The *students* came to learn. But they knew that they weren't going to be taught the content of a particular unit on the particular course which they were studying. They had signed on for a day in which they would concentrate on developing generalizable and transferable abilities, which were expected to prove relevant to their continuing learning in science. In contrast, the quintet of *tutors* came to this residential event to develop, with my assistance, their competence to tutor transferable skills in second-level science studies. They had with them five invited *visitors*, who were also (with one exception) science tutors, but who were tutors who had had no contact with this project previously. These visitors came to be observers, co-counsellors and (on a few occasions) peers whose questions and comments could catalytically facilitate development for the 'Inverness Five'. Finally there were two *staff developers*. One (me) was charged to support the quintet of tutors; the other (a newcomer to this area of activity) came to facilitate the activities for the five visitors.

Academic staff development is itself a form of adult learning and education. The adults concerned simply happen to be tutors or teachers, whose particular subject or discipline is higher education. The content of that subject ranges from pedagogy to the development of personal, cognitive and interpersonal abilities. I see no reason to suspect that these adults should learn any differently, in principle, from the adult students whom they tutor. That is why it seemed to me eminently apt that both groups at the residential events I have described should have been set up to progress around the Kolb cycle, and should have been deliberately and purposefully facilitated in so doing. It was my intention, then, that the two central groups would spend the weekend following the Kolb cycle, although in different ways and from different starting points.

The students were to be taken into the (upper) cycle in Figure 9.1 from their *experiences* in science studies in the recent past. Starting from there, we hoped that they would find themselves able to begin to identify the transferable skills which were commonly demanded of them; and then, more analytically and in more detail, to spell out precisely what these skills should entail. After that, they would be encouraged, in interactive pairings, to test out the generalizations which should now have emerged from that initial reflection, and to consider their relevance to any further and similar experiences which their co-counselling student partner could volunteer and describe. At the end of the day, they should leave the entire sequence of activity ready to test out, in their own further experiences of the next month or so, the transferable skills of which they were now nearly aware or had a keener perception. We were confident that they would continue to be encouraged to reflect on their use of these skills, since they were students who would be tutored throughout the year by one of the Inverness Five. In the event, we were to prove successful in achieving these ambitious outcomes for the students.

The tutors, of course, had a longer programme. This ran from the Friday evening until the Sunday lunch time. It opened on the first evening with the input of a generalization, presented as a reprise in a fishbowl situation – where we who were actively discussing and planning were sitting at the centre, inside the 'bowl', and the others sat outside, looking in, and doing no more than observing at that

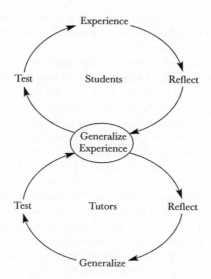

Figure 9.1   Kolb cycles interrelated

time. The Inverness Five and I rehearsed what they meant by, and how they would explain, transferable cognitive skills for second-level science; what an awareness of these could imply; and how they believed that that awareness could be nurtured. This was a true rehearsal, for the events of the next day focused on the student–tutor interaction which was now going through its final preparation, which the visitors were there to observe. In so doing, the tutors revisited (and thus declared) some of the principles which we had forged in our reflections together, as a group, and would use with, and explain to, the students:

- They would use no special jargon, and would go to considerable lengths to employ *everyday language.*
- They would introduce and explain the concepts which they needed through *examples.* This included their descriptions of particular transferable skills and their general definition of 'transferable skill'.
- They would not specify in formal terms any tasks which they set for the students, their tutors or their visiting colleagues. Instead they simply *demonstrated* what they wanted people to do, and invited these people to imitate, and 'do that kind of thing', but with different subject matter or in a different situation.
- Instead of letting the students and their colleagues concentrate on the refinement and perfecting of generalizations, they would encourage a speedy move to the *testing* of a first draft generalization, on another example or in another experience.

In the second part of that first evening, having explained their concepts and their pedagogy to the visitors, the quintet came out of the fishbowl and went into pairings, each with a visitor. Each pair talked through the details of the programme for the next day, in which the visitors were usually to be observers, while the tutors put their plans to the test.

On the next day, which has been described in fuller detail elsewhere (Cowan, 1994), the tutors took the student learners, in pairs as I have explained, around the Kolb cycle – beginning from experiences of learning in science where transferable skills were, or should have been, relevant. The visitors observed, and at times came together to discuss what they had been seeing and hearing. They reported back to the tutors on their generalized comments and conclusions. As the day progressed, some of the visitors (unfortunately) found it impossible to adhere to their negotiated role, and succumbed to the urge to join in the increasingly informal discussions between a tutor and the corresponding pair of students.

Before the students departed at the end of the afternoon, they completed an evaluative questionnaire whose analysis proved embarrassingly fulsome and positive, while at the same time being powerfully convincing and objective. This was complemented by an evaluative plenary in an unusual format, which was designed to extract extremes in the range of feedback. The visitors gathered together to review the day holistically. The tutors, who had planned to reflect in the same way, instead engaged involuntarily in an important de-briefing of an affective nature. They had been very conscious of the risks they were taking and the uncertainty, for them, which had been presented by the unfamiliar situation, 24 hours previously. The undoubted success of the event, while in one sense an enormous relief, was at the same time a massive release from tension. We surely need to acknowledge more openly (and more frequently) the anxiety associated with innovative risk-taking – and its immediate outcomes.

You should note that, for the tutors and to some extent for the visitors, the Kolb cycle (in the lower part of Figure 9.1) began from a different starting point. It commenced in the *generalizations* which the tutors played through on the Friday evening, and which had been an input from me, many months before. It continued into their plans for *testing* out these generalizations in the events of the Saturday; and it rolled forward into these *particular experiences*, on which tutors and visitors were beginning to *reflect* by the end of the working day, on the Saturday.

I had intended that, after a relaxing Saturday evening, the work of the Sunday morning would concentrate first on further generalizing from the experiences and reflections of the weekend, and would then progress into the formulation of plans for future tutorial activity. But it didn't quite work out that way. I discovered that tutors, perhaps more than the visitors, needed more time than I had allowed for their reflection before they felt ready to proceed to generalization – let alone planning and development. Nevertheless, two of the visitors volunteered that their part in the weekend, which I had merely hoped would be facilitative for the Inverness Five, had moved them to plan distinct changes in their own immediate tutorial activity.

This long account describes only the beginning of an even longer staff development journey for two of the Inverness Five. Twelve months later, in January 1995, Helen Wood and Claire Geddes accompanied me as staff developers, to an event in Jutland, for Aalborg University in Denmark. This had been planned because Mona Dahms, a member of staff there, had been enthused by the description (along the lines I have just given), which I had presented to the conference in Gothenburg in June 1994.

The Aalborg pilot also followed the double-Kolb cycle in Figure 9.1, though on a much larger scale – both in terms of numbers and the duration of the (bilingual) event. It involved some 15 tutors and 25 students, in a programme which was of almost a week's duration for the tutors, and two days less than that for the students. Anxiety levels, for all three of us Scots, were again high – but the risks brought their associated reward, for they took us into situations with distinctly creative possibilities, with some valued outcomes in due course. The pilot led to radical developments for students of technology in the Basic Education Year in Aalborg, with the result that about 460 students and over 100 staff were engaged in the derivative activity in January 1996. However, it is with the beginnings for the Inverness Five that this example has really been concerned, so I will focus only on that meantime, and take the Aalborg story no further in these pages.

Comment

Throughout this convoluted arrangement of developmental activities, mismatches emerged again and again for consideration – as promptings which encouraged tutors to try to teach differently. There were the initial mismatches between the learning experiences as students had reported them through IPR, and as the tutor concerned had perceived it. This type of informative feedback had disturbed and fascinated Helen Wood, who was to go on from it to recruit the Inverness Five. Then there were the mismatches between what that quintet had hoped for in their routine tutorials, and what they judged to be actually happening, in terms of learning experiences and learning outcomes which they identified through illuminative evaluation. These were the mismatches which had prompted us to go into retreat, to experiment and to consolidate progress. There were also the mismatches which the visitors to the residential event had perceived and discussed – which were principally discrepancies between the aspirations of the Inverness Five and the more traditional aspirations of the visitors.

It could be argued that it was perception of, and reflection on, mismatches which most effectively and frequently motivated the tutorial staff to progress around the cycle, and to seek out, to experiment with and to evaluate, alternative methods of tutoring, with alternative goals.

Equally, however, it will not have escaped you that the Inverness Five drew on, and built on, much in the form of initiating input from me. For it was I who had first suggested the elements of a pedagogy which they applied to their own development and to their students' learning. It was I who first tabled the Rogerian approach to teaching and learning, to a group of tutors which had included Helen Wood. The Five subsequently looked to me for suggestions to assist them in their planning to test out their new ideas, and in structuring their reflections. My suggestions were invited and warmly received; but it was understood between us that I left the quintet with their autonomy, the exercise of which was to prove a powerful influence on their development. I was glad that we collaborated in this way. For I believe fervently that the most worthwhile development is tutor-facilitated yet learner-directed. This example tends to endorse that belief, I hope.

The Inverness Five and I learned a lot together. Together we created what was, for our institution (and, later, for Aalborg), a totally different type of staff development activity. Together, in our different ways and with our different levels of experience and ability, we dreamt up ideas for teaching and learning which none of us had ever thought of before. So it will not have escaped you that I, too, was following my own Kolb cycle. In this, I relied to a considerable extent on those below me in the pyramid, that Inverness quintet, to assist *me*, with *my* reflection. Helen Wood shared with me, for example, in planning how we would test out my next generalization, as I emerged from the apparent disaster of the first residential event and eventually progressed in the sequence which led three of us to Aalborg – and beyond.

It is also important to recognize that we six shared not only in our failures and disappointments but also in our successes. Our group session, at the end of that successful Saturday when we were separate from the visitors, was one of the most intense experiences of my career in staff development. Equally, the sheer feeling of success, after a period of acute personal risk in the Aalborg event of January 1995, was both a bond and a source of strength for Helen, Claire and myself. Consequently I conclude this example with two questions for you which epitomize for me some elements of this account, and some features of innovative teaching:

Should a teacher who sets out to facilitate reflection aspire to progress constantly through situations which involve real risk and anxiety? Are these an essential part of the teaching experience, providing the stimulus to ensure freshness, rigour, and a keen application to task on the part of the tutor?

To what extent is there a correlation between depth of fellowship with one's teaching and learning peers, and the depth of reflection which professional dialogue with them can provoke? Is it really possible to self-facilitate deep and thorough reflection, in isolation or with detachment?

And that leads me on to a longer list of questions, taken from this chapter as a whole.

Questions to prompt your reflection

I can summarize a number of facilitative questions from some of the lessons which I believe emerge from these examples. These are questions on which I would encourage you to ponder – and for which I hope you will find your own answers, rather than expect me to offer you mine. Here are my questions, then, in italics after somewhat rambling preambles:

- It is a singularly British characteristic to tie staff and curriculum development firmly to discipline areas. Even when chemists are put together, one will almost certainly protest that he is an organic chemist, whereas she is an inorganic chemist. In other countries, and in my experience notably both in Sweden and in the Middle East, academics protest volubly if they are denied the richness of mixing professionally with colleagues from radically different disciplines, with and from whom they feel they can profitably learn a great deal.

  In your own self-directed development as a university teacher, do you make sufficient efforts to establish working contacts with academics in disciplines other than your own?

- In my own learning about how to develop analytical ability, I have found my encounters with classicists and historians more profitable than with any other academics. Again, while serving my apprenticeship with regard to the design of tutorless group activities with higher level cognitive goals, I have borrowed more from sociology and social work departments than from any others. In other words, I have often found that good teaching approaches which I have encountered in other discipline areas can readily be translated into a form suitable for use by me and my students – with less demand on my ingenuity and time than if I had needed to invent something from scratch.

  Are you mining enough from some of the rich seams of educational practice which are available to you in other disciplines?

- As a young engineer, I quickly learned that it was commendable and systematic to design in an iterative manner, constantly refining and improving and changing, until the end result had been optimized. As an innovative university teacher, I found myself in an environment where most of my colleagues, though fortunately not my head of department, thought that an educational innovation or change should be something which is decided upon, planned – and finally delivered in what should immediately prove to be virtually its final form.

Perhaps it is because of frailty on my part that I have never managed to get things right first time; or perhaps it is as true in education as in engineering, that a systematic and iterative approach to design represents sound practice. Certainly most of my educational innovations have had to go through several iterations, with increasing sample size and less resource expended per student. Only after that have I felt prepared to offer something which could be evaluated competitively against the status quo. My 'Course without a Syllabus' (Cowan, 1980b) was no worse than the status quo on its first iteration. But it took me five iterations of refinement before I was prepared, and felt justified (Cowan, 1986a), to offer the final result for external summative evaluation and assessment.

When you innovate, are you sufficiently prepared to iterate on the basis of formative evaluations?

- When my student problem-solvers had produced their lengthy audio-tapes containing recorded protocols (Example 9.1), which neither the available resource nor the motivation of the staff could sustain, I came to the conclusion that my secretary couldn't transcribe them, and that I couldn't find time to analyse them. So it was obvious to me that the job must be done in a different way. That was why I thought of getting the students to do the analysis. And that fortuitous change certainly paid off for me, and for them, in its powerful consequences.

In innovatory development, do you simply accept a negative as indicating that there is 'No through road', or do you consciously go out of your way to do what is virtually the opposite of that which didn't work, to get something which does work?

Generalizations

In my first draft of this chapter, I was content to point out that, in my examples, the most common way for university teachers to find useful support when they set out to innovate in their teaching has been identified in terms of personal contacts. These may be contacts, in person or in print, with someone a bit further down that same road, who can share experiences, ideas and suggestions, and who can encourage and act as a sort of mentor – for a while, at least. This type of association should lead quickly into the testing out of the new ideas, first on a small scale and perhaps in partnership with a mentor or close colleague who (in effect) co-counsels. Such experimentation may begin by imitating and adapting something which has already been shown to work, in someone else's hands. But after that it probably entails going on to do things rather differently, after reflection which takes account of the talents and ideas of you (as the new innovator), and the significant features of your situation and discipline.

On reflection, this generalization still disappoints me. For I know that there are other strong and common messages which can be identified in my examples. Since I'm sure you will be determined to formulate your own conclusions and generalizations, whatever I write, I will freely table my new list of some of the factors which emerge for me from this chapter. These are:

- taking risks;
- iterating;
- in any pilot, entering into a partnership with the students concerned;
- the almost evangelical impact of some innovatory personalities;
- basing what you attempt on your beliefs about what matters in learning, and for learners;
- watching out for mismatches, and reacting positively to them;
- turning mistakes into positive lessons learned;
- benefiting from reflecting on teaching, as much as getting learners to benefit from reflecting about learning;
- using inputs from those with experience, once a first declaration of interest has been made;
- experiencing teaching and learning situations as a learner, especially when these are unfamiliar or novel;
- publishing accounts of innovation;
- repeating previous research or development studies, in your own field;
- formative evaluations verging on action-research, with students joining in interpreting the lessons to be learned for development;
- partnerships with kindred spirits who are not necessarily experts in the field, which lead on to valuable cooperation;
- cross-disciplinary transfer of ideas and contacts;
- experimentation off one's own territory, where it is easier to recover from failure!
- (from some of the examples elsewhere in this text) being almost Machiavellian in the activity outlines you devise, in order to achieve certain learning outcomes or even win space to attempt them;
- being tactical in relations with colleagues and institutions;
- making provision to develop the developer, in all of this;
- being prepared to get it wrong.

You will no doubt have your own views about that list. I hope so!

So, have any of the odysseys which I have described contained something that may prove helpful on the way ahead for you? Would you regard this text and your reading of it, for example, as sufficient generalized input for you to begin your testing; or would you still need more support from a mentor or partner?

Before you test this, some second thoughts from me

1. Is it not a pedagogy of affective influence, rather than an interpretation of the Kolb cycle, which will best describe what happened in the important opening stages of the examples in this chapter? Is the key issue not 'what would persuade me, or you, to try something different?'
2. Is it at all valid to think in terms of the Kolb cycle, in situations where the important decisions and/or outcome are essentially affective?

3. In the examples described, the outcomes of the various personal contacts and readings were decisions to try out a new idea, or to rely on the experience of another, or to follow an example. These are primarily affective decisions, concerned with motivation and commitment and a willingness to innovate and take risks. They are not at that point identifiable as the development of abilities or the acquiring of deep conceptual understanding. To be sure, cognitive outcomes are also significant in my personal development stories. But is that not a consequence, chronologically, of primary decisions made initially in the affective domain – and made either because someone came to accept a philosophy of teaching and learning or because they valued the experience and success of particular tutors or staff development personalities? Is the emphasis on changing values something that distinguishes staff development from other forms of adult education?

4. Feelings and attitudes and the allaying of anxieties are clearly very important in developing a new approach to the design of learning and teaching situations, and in the choice of learning objectives. How can they best be catered for?

5. Should any teacher have the impertinence to try to encourage others to change their approaches?

6. If so, what might be the elements of that staff development pedagogy – and should we not think more about the issue of persuasion in situations where – as Bob Matthew hinted – we want our students to take up our goals, beliefs and convictions, and learn together with us accordingly?

7. Are the three types of teaching in the following quotation notably different, or fundamentally the same?

> No teacher I of boys or smaller fry,
> No teacher I of teachers, no, not I,
> Mine was the distant aim, the longer reach,
> To teach men how to teach men how to teach.

(Ramsay, 1956)

8. Finally, should you give in to second or even third thoughts about the risks of innovation? Or do you, like me, believe that it is only as the lead husky that you will each day enjoy varied and rewarding prospects?

Dear John

I'm sure that you will agree that we owe it to our students to be systematic and responsible when we make any changes in our educational systems and in their objective.

If I'm going to follow you down this reflective practitioner road, I will want to set in place thorough arrangements for what you have called evaluation. First, I will want to identify the need and scope for curricular improvement in what I am already doing, and in anything new which I try out. At the same time I will want to plan for summative evaluation which will objectively compare what I devise with the status quo – and will tell me, as well as the world, if what I am doing is sound and valid.

Can I do that, in everyday situations, without becoming or hiring an educational researcher? How should such innovations be evaluated?

10

How Can Such Innovations
Be Evaluated?

Introduction

This chapter begins with a set of eight examples, describing methods which have served me well, but do not exhaust the possibilities for evaluation. At the drafting stage, I felt I should divide these into formative and summative groups – but it wasn't quite as simple as that, I discovered. For many of the methods which I have used to confirm that I have achieved what I set out to do, and are hence summative evaluations, have also provided suggestions about how to improve, which made them formative. I have therefore begun here with examples which were at least in part summative in that they provided evidence for me and others of the learning outcomes – and then I have gone on to examples which more and more take a formative form. But be on the lookout for the possibility of formative outcomes from the early examples, into the bargain.

Then a few other examples, a brief generalization, and second thoughts to leave you thinking.

Example 10.1: Finding out about learning, using pre-tests and post-tests

In my early attempts to develop qualitative understanding through reflection on examples and subsequent generalization (Cowan and Morton, 1973; Cowan, 1974a, 1974b), I created a range of teaching and learning situations which were participative, novel and intended to be intrinsically motivating. My students tended to respond positively, although I was always left wondering if that reaction arose from the novelty rather than from the effectiveness of the activities I had designed. My concern was to know whether or not the activities improved performance, both in respect of tasks which were either already a demand of the curriculum, and for the new objectives which often I was introducing.

In many cases it was a relatively simple matter to construct two test papers which each presented that type of task in a comparable setting and, to the best of my ability, with a comparable level of demand. I could divide my class by past performance into two reasonably matched groups, giving test paper A to one group and test paper B to the other – before they began on the reflective activity. Both papers should then yield similar pre-test marks. After the students emerged from their reflective activity, or a week later if I wished to be assured of retention and consolidation, the first group could tackle test paper B with the second group tackling test paper A. (See also, for instance, Example 10.2.)

It was thereafter a fairly simple matter to determine statistically if there had been an improvement, if the two test papers were comparable instruments of enquiry, and if there was any evidence of task transfer which might have contaminated that comparison. This approach provided a summative evaluation of the learning, in relation to the predetermined objectives on which the tests focused.

Example 10.2: Finding out about progress, from dynamic lists of questions

Two facilitative lecturers planned a series of half-day events in which students should develop, through reflection on experience, certain cognitive abilities which the tutors considered important in their subject area. The lecturers made the assumption that they would be able to judge the overall impact of this programme from the students' subsequent performances in examinations. They also felt that they could themselves judge the general competence of the students and compare it with the work of similar students in previous years, when there had been no special programme devoted to the development of abilities. However, the lecturers were aware that factors other than tuition can influence learning and development, and they were alive to that confounding factor. So they also wished to know what immediate impact the various components of each new half-day programme would have on the development of the students.

They asked me to evaluate each half-day thoroughly. I devised a plan which I was later to refine (Cowan and George, 1992b). Before the three-part event began, each student completed a simple proforma, on which as learners they had listed the questions with which they hoped to make progress in their learning during the course of the event. These lists of questions were credited against a pseudonym, and taken in for photocopying. The lecturers also arranged that the students took a pre-test and later a post-test (Example 10.1), which concentrated on the declared learning objectives.

At the end of the first discrete component of the programme, the students retrieved their own question sheet, and amended it – so that it would now represent their outstanding personal agenda for the remainder of the event. Where the student deemed learning to have occurred, some questions were deleted; sometimes questions were added, when new needs had become apparent. The sheets were taken in again, and photocopied a second time. After the next component, the sheets were once more returned to the students for amendment, and again collected by the lecturers for photocopying. Quickly the teaching staff were made aware of the progress of learning, and planned their activity in the third section of the event accordingly. There was thus a strong incentive to persuade learners to identify outstanding needs, and not to record and return needs which had been met already. At the end of the programme, the procedure was repeated.

Three sources of illuminative information were thus available to the lecturers. First of all, they had a clear listing of the aspirations and expectations which were in the students' minds, at the beginning of the event. Secondly, from the questions which had been scored out at the various stages in the programme, they had an account from the students of the outcomes which the students perceived that part of the event to have achieved for them. The lecturers could check that perception, to some extent, against the students' subsequent performance in the pre-test/post-test comparison, although that could only be done on a group basis, as the anonymity of the reporting had rendered individual correlations impossible. Finally, and in some ways the most thought-provoking of all, the lecturers were able to obtain the learners' impression of the element in the programme which had written off declared questions, or had provoked new questions.

Programme revision was informed by this data, which the lecturers judged in the light of their expectations and considered criteria. The method above all provided a summative account of the learning outcomes from each component of the programme, and of the learning expectations for the class group.

Example 10.3: A method for summative evaluation facilitates learning

It had long worried me that students of engineering may learn little more than to carry out calculations, of whose meaning and significance they are really unaware. One example of this is apparent in exercises which involve the calculation of what are called second moments of area. Sadly it is possible, and indeed convenient, to set out these calculations in a tabular form which virtually eliminates the need for thought. Hence, given a cross-section which can be divided into geometrical shapes having positive or negative area, the position of the centroid and the magnitude of the second moment of area can be calculated methodically and with no use of, or dependence on, understanding of what is being done.

Some time ago, almost by chance, I invented a style of test question which evaluated the acquisition of the qualitative and conceptual understanding that I valued, in this context as indeed in others (Cowan, 1982). This understanding had not hitherto featured in the traditional hidden curriculum, as conveyed to students by assessment in the form of the numerical type of question and task I have just described.

I used my new type of question for evaluating the effectiveness of my teaching. I presented students with a number of familiar shapes, with certain dimensions in common. None of the shapes had dimensions given for them, though sometimes I used algebraic symbols to indicate relative values. It would have been an appallingly complex process to calculate positions of centroids and second moments of area using these algebraic symbols – and any others which the student might choose to add to my diagrams.

The type of task which I had invented asked the student to list the shapes in ascending order of second moment of area – where that was possible, and giving reasons to justify the order they had chosen. Where it was not possible to include one or more shapes on the basis of the information given, the student should justify their omission from the ascending order list. Studies of the problem-solving using recorded protocols, as described in Example 9.1, demonstrated that the demand of the task could not be met by calculations in numbers or in algebraic symbols. For this type of question, as opposed to the more traditional numerical form, can only be answered by displaying (in the reasoning contained in the justifications) an understanding of the concepts of centre of area and of second moment of area. I have since shown (Cowan, 1986a) that similar types of question, for completely different problem areas, can insist on this same level of conceptual understanding. This I have similarly confirmed from recorded protocols of the students' problem-solving. That confirmation having been obtained, the ascending order question can then become a method of checking summatively for conceptual understanding, or a task for a tutorial situation – or both.

I designed a new type of test item, then, to provide in the first instance a vehicle for the summative evaluation of qualitative understanding. But it soon became both a new type of examination question and a tutorial means of developing understanding, because it provided a structure for discussion between learners about fundamental concepts. It is interesting to note in passing that the format devised in Example 10.2 also became transformed into a format for teaching and learning – in that case into a structure for an interactive tutorial. This is indeed typical of many of the formats devised for formative evaluation, as witnessed in the useful texts by Cross and colleagues (Angelo and Cross, 1993; Cross and Steadman, 1996).

Example 10.4: Finding out about learning, using questionnaires

In my early days as a university lecturer, I encountered an excellent Australian questionnaire which enabled students to provide feedback on the lectures they had been given. I had copies made, explained my purpose to my students, and issued these sheets one morning to one of my classes, to be completed anonymously and returned before they left the lecture theatre. I collected the piles of forms from the ends of the rows, and took them home – to read them privately.

The feedback was reasonably encouraging – until I came to one form which puzzled me. Like the majority of the returns I had read up to that point, this one informed me that I had mannerisms, and that they were sometimes slightly amusing; but fortunately, like the others, it reassured me that my mannerisms were not really distracting. Then it volunteered, in handwriting which happily I did not recognize, that 'this lecturer eats chalk'. This struck me as a flippant and unhelpful comment – until I came to another in similar form, and yet another which offered much the same feedback. It was clear that these students had not been sitting near to each other. I was reading independent comments, with the same remarkable message.

It was remarkable because I know that I hate even the feeling of chalk on my fingers, which at that time I frequently accumulated as I lectured, since chalkboards were still in use. I would definitely abhor the contact of chalk with my lips or my tongue. Clearly I had a mannerism which made me appear as if I was eating chalk – a mannerism of which I had no sooner learned than I immediately desired to eradicate it. And so in its place I quickly developed a curious and evasive mannerism. Whenever I was conscious of my hand moving from my side, and up towards my face, I whipped it smartly down to the vertical position again. That noteworthy and idiosyncratic flailing action was not a valuable outcome from this questionnaire enquiry.

Nevertheless, I went on using questionnaires – even after I was well into resource-based learning and seldom in the position of speaking to a complete class. In Scotland, it has long been the custom that the professor lectures to the first year. Consequently, despite my commitment to individualized learning, I was called on to take six lectures at the beginning of the first year, with a class who naturally did not know me, and for whom I had to introduce one of the main curriculum topics.

At the end of my six lectures, I took some time to issue (as in the previous example) a simple questionnaire on lecturing, which was completed by ticking boxes or by circling one number on a Likert (five-point) scale. Unfortunately I didn't allow quite enough time for this operation. As a result, only a third of the class managed to complete the last section – which dealt with my use of the overhead projector. However, from this part-sample I was delighted to learn that my acetates had been clear, that I had not obscured the image with my body, that I had left the acetates on the projector for long enough to allow the class to assimilate them, and that these acetates contained neither too much nor too little information. It will not surprise you that I was pleased with this feedback – although it will perhaps surprise you to know why I was pleased. I was pleased because, as the sceptic I have explicitly declared myself to be about the reliability of questionnaire returns, I now had good reason to endorse in public my private scepticism. For I had not used the overhead projector once during these six lectures.

Please bear with me a little longer as I tell you about one further example in justification of my distrust of questionnaires. It concerns a situation in 1971, when the Cement and Concrete Association put on sale sets of slides and lecture notes, for use in universities and colleges. I decided to assemble tape-slide sequences using these slides, and based my commentary heavily on the published notes. I arranged for my tape-slide sequences to be viewed by small groups of students, and prompted them to engage in informal discussion once the programmes had finished.

As the students emerged from their group rooms, I asked them for their feedback. This was positive. They stressed with enthusiasm that this was a good way to learn, and that I should do more on the same lines. They were happy to complete a brief questionnaire which I gave them, and warmly affirmed that informal verdict. Thereafter, I gave them a simple little test – to be completed anonymously. I explained that this was a 90/90 test – one in whose ten questions I would expect 90 per cent of the class to score nine correct answers from ten questions. With obvious confidence and optimism, my students sat down to tackle the test – returning the papers five minutes later with long faces. 'John, I know I should be able to answer these questions – they're quite fair, and the sequence covered them. But I can't remember many of the answers.' The evidence of the test paper did not coincide with the evidence of the questionnaire, nor with the 'gut reaction' of the students. I've never since trusted someone who tells me about their judgements based on gut reactions, unless they can tell me how they distinguish between gut reactions and indigestion.

I caution you to find a moral in these three anecdotes. In my experience, questionnaires can be a useful instrument of enquiry, provided we are aware of their limitations. Questionnaires will often suggest questions which should be asked and pursued, or issues which should be explored. But, on their own and without corroboration, they can yield misleading or incorrect, although sincere, advice; because they tend to be reports of opinions, which require to be substantiated, and not of facts on which we can rely.

The great strength of professionally designed questionnaire studies as a research method comes when they are used after much qualitative research has been undertaken, so that we know enough about individual experience and can encapsulate that in the wording and choice of the questions. The quantitative coverage of whole populations or large samples of students then allows us to judge what weight to give to each of the diverse reactions to our teaching, and provides guidance for change. Questionnaires can be a helpful tool in formative evaluations under these conditions.

Example 10.5: Finding out about process, by observing behaviour

I made a major change in the way I presented a design task to a first year class, who were to plan, fabricate and test a number of balsawood model structures. I had worried that, in the past, groups had not tackled this task according to what I saw as 'good design practice'. Despite the advice and best endeavours of myself and my colleagues, our students had spent little time in dreaming up a range of options, and in critically comparing their strengths and weaknesses. They had not even devoted much effort to an analysis of the brief, out of which should have emerged their ideas for successful designs. At that time, and even today, analysis – in my judgement – is the neglected skill in engineering education, and practice (Cowan, 1986b). Rather than analysing, my students had immediately rushed, like Gadarene swine who believe themselves at the forefront of progress, into an ill-conceived plan and the construction of an ineffective structure.

So I changed the task. Previously the students had been given a brief, and asked to design and fabricate a structure which would be tested – with marks awarded in a norm-referenced assessment according to its performance under load, in competition with the models produced by groups of fellow students. But my new assessment demand, in truly Machiavellian style, required them to produce *two* models which satisfied the brief, but which were distinct and so must embody features which were significantly different. They were told that they would be awarded their marks according to the performance of the poorer of their two models. Thus, I hoped, they would be encouraged to analyse the brief, and to think about how to generate two competitive and distinct responses to it, in a manner more akin to the process which is followed by a thoughtful designer, for whom analysis and creative consideration of competitive options precedes any decision for action.

I evaluated this change pragmatically – but validly, I believe. During their modelling coursework in my own university, I carefully observed and recorded certain changes in my students' behaviour, in comparison with that of students in previous years. I did the same when I entered teams of first year students to compete in a prestigious structural modelling competition for students from the universities throughout Scotland. My first year teams competed there against third and final year teams from elsewhere. I will report here only on the second of my comparisons, since the observations and messages to be drawn from them were much the same as in the first, but more quickly assembled.

In the setting of the national competition, two stark discrepancies were immediately apparent between the behaviour of my teams, and that of the others. Both changes could be quantified. The first was that my teams spent a greater amount of time than did the others in preparatory thinking and discussion – before they reached a decision about the model they would build (for, in the national competition, only one model was built). The second was the greater amount of time which they spent in comparing options, before they decided on their final choice or choices. (This was a subset of the first time measured, of course.)

In the national competition, the able students from the third and fourth years of the other universities had decided on the model form, and had commenced fabrication, within 10–15 minutes. After 40 minutes, my first year students were still discussing and deliberating. At that point a colleague from a neighbouring university came across to point out to me, tactfully, how lost and out of their depth my unfortunate young students obviously were, and how embarrassed they would be as the evening progressed. He suggested we should find an easy way out for them. His worries were compounded when he noted the time which they spent ponderously deliberating over the options which they had identified as being open to them, once they had eventually emerged from their creative brainstorming. As a result, he commented, they were spending three times as long on group discussion as did the other teams. I gently reassured him that the blame, if there was to be a blame, would be mine, and that I would conscientiously shoulder it when the time came to do so; I pointed out that, in any case, there was little that we could now do at this late stage, without causing more embarrassment than we sought to avoid.

Two hours or so later his fears were proved groundless, and his reflections on process were jolted, when one of my first year teams won the competition – and the other came third. My observations (of both the competition and of that entire class group in comparison with their predecessors) described behaviour in norm-referenced terms, and provided some information for my further use, which was therefore (in part) formative evaluation. However, I felt that the competition result was primarily a convincing summative evaluation of the changed teaching strategy I had followed, although I recognized that the sample was small. The result thus provided some reassurance about learning outcomes – although there could, of course, have been other explanations of the students' success. Counting and measuring can provide helpful evaluative data without requiring much effort or subtlety on the part of the evaluator.

Example 10.6: Finding out about process, from a spoken protocol

One of my colleagues in a Department of Mathematics produced some computer-assisted learning materials which set out to convey meaningful conceptual under-standing to first year learners. That understanding was to be applied in problem-solving situations, with the aim of developing the appropriate abilities. He was anxious to find out the impact his materials and their presentation were having on the students' thinking.

I arranged to meet with trios of students, over and after an informal buffet lunch, in his small staff room which contained a PC. When the students were ready to work, we booted up the computer and set the program in action. One student sat at the keyboard, and began to work with the learning materials in the normal way – but at my request she talked out her thoughts aloud as she did so. The other two students, one at each of her shoulders, were told firmly that they were not to engage in discussion. They were charged by me to ask her questions, so that they would be able to carry on, just as she was doing, if she were called away to the telephone. They were not to offer assistance or advice. They were not to discuss her actions or compare what she was doing with the ways in which they themselves would have tackled the tasks, had they been on their own. They were simply to ask questions so that they could empathize with her approach. I explained that, in so doing, they would incidentally extract further information from her about why she did things, as well as about how she did them.

After a little while, they changed positions. One of the men sat in the chair and worked on the keyboard, while the woman and the other man questioned from the other positions, and worked in the same way as hitherto. And so too, in due course, with the third student problem-solver.

Thereafter we engaged in a four-way discussion. This brought me into the pic-ture for the first time, as I had so far been standing somewhat detached from all of this, unobtrusively making my notes of what they had been doing and describing to each other. I summed up what I had heard of the processes followed by each of the three students, checked these summaries for accuracy and completeness, and with the students' help compared and contrasted their three approaches. I tried at the same time to transfer what I was extracting into a generalized form, which I even-tually reported back to the author of the computer software. He responded to the feedback accordingly, and in his own way – by finding out how many students in the class could identify with the points I reported to him.

Much of the data I obtained confirmed my colleague's previous design decisions or influenced future ones. Some revealed striking mismatches between his assump-tions and expectations on the one hand, and the reality of student preference or performance on the other. This was particularly so in respect of the range of individual responses and differences.

I have used this method on several occasions with computer-assisted learning, in subject areas from mathematics to languages.

Example 10.7: Finding out about process by lurking, and interviewing

Several Open University science tutors (Example 9.4) had decided to change the priorities in their tutorial teaching, including the tutorials which they delivered to isolated students through telephone conference calls. They intended that these audio-conferences would now concentrate more on the development of abilities than, as hitherto, on the mastery of content.

This group of tutors held a preparatory meeting. They resolved to set up arrangements in which – with the full knowledge and agreement of the students concerned – one of the tutors would 'lurk' on a conference call, listening into what was said but not contributing in any way, other than to say 'Hello' at the beginning, when their presence on line was mentioned. After the call was finished, the lurker would phone two students (who had been warned of this arrangement) to ask each in turn a number of carefully selected and planned questions, seeking information about what they had learned during the conference call – and how that had come about.

In this way, while the call was still fresh in the memory of the students, and without the introduction of unduly obtrusive technology or methodology, the lurker was able to extract recall of excerpts of the learning experience, for particular students.

This data either confirmed or disappointed the tutor's expectations. There were some informative mismatches between the perceptions of the call by students, and by the tutor. All information (much of which was confirmatory) was fed back to the tutor, who reacted to that as she wished. In some cases, the tutor went to other students in the group, to check that this feedback was typical of their experience. In other cases, the tutor changed the style of at least parts of the event, on the occasion of the next conference call. Sometimes the tutor would opt to ask questions generally of the group within the next conference call, where she called for the detailed feedback she needed, on which to base her revisions of her strategy and style.

Example 10.8: Finding out about learning, from reflective learning journals

Following a week of IDS activity (Example 2.3) which had concentrated on problem-solving, I extracted and analysed the accounts which students gave in their learning journals of their reflections and progress.

One student wrote of a wonderful problem-solving method which he claimed he had devised. He wrote in a complex style and gave a condensed description of his methodology. By the last few lines of the first page of his description, he had left me without any understanding of what it was that he, the learner, was describing, and without a single positive idea on my part for a supportive comment. In my role as commentator, I worried over this for some time. Never, in my previous experience with learning journals, had I left as significant a page as this without a single comment. Yet, in all honesty, and with my commitment to an approach according to Rogers (Rogers, 1961), I could not think of any non-judgemental or non-directive comment to add to that script. For my reaction – starkly – was one of total incomprehension of what the student was writing, and hence of complete lack of empathy with the message which may have been contained therein.

After agonizing, I decided to maintain my integrity and refrain from commenting. With a feeling of acute embarrassment at this implicit inadequacy on my part, I turned over the page to encounter the top lines on the page in which he had written 'I don't expect the first page meant anything to you – but it means a lot to me.' I confess that, at this point, I found myself fervently wishing that this helpful comment had been written at the foot of the first page, and not at the beginning of the second page. The student journal-writer continued, by describing how this obscure (and to me still totally incomprehensible) problem-solving method had been applied by him to various activities in the second half of the study week – with remarkable success.

This journal-writer next recounted how it had occurred to him that, if this method was valid for the situations which he encountered in his studies, perhaps it might also be valid for the rather different difficulties which he encountered in his part-time engagement as a Scout leader, with two inept assistants. There followed another page or so of journal entry, in which the student narrated his account of how the same method, still incomprehensible to me as the journal-reader, had been applied to the difficult situation in his Scout troop. And there, as in the writer's undergraduate studies, it had apparently led to a successful outcome which the journal-writer reported in some (convincing) detail.

All of this spread out into an entry of nine or ten pages. At the end of these, in a cryptic and business-like conclusion, the journal-writer said that he didn't really expect that any of this would be terribly meaningful to the reader. 'But it's meaningful to me. It has worked for me in a variety of situations, and I'm sure it's going to work for me next week as well. I know I've written far more in this journal entry than you wanted from me – but it's been a very exciting and successful week, and I wanted to tell somebody about it.'

This, like other journal entries in that particular week, provided subjective and possibly distorted first-hand evidence of positive outcomes which the journal-writers judged to have been 'successes' as far as they were concerned, in response to the ideas encountered in the IDS activity of that week. Being someone who taught this student and his fellows in class and group work, I could and did make some indirect checks of the authenticity of the claims which he made in his journal.

Triangulation is certainly important, as I hope I established in Example 10.2. Equally, we must sometimes face up to the fact that the ease of obtaining and verifying evaluative data is often inversely proportional to its usefulness and meaningfulness. The evaluative innovator must strive for an optimum balance.

Other examples

Data is often generated, but not assembled or analysed, I regret to say. Embedded in the structure of the teaching and learning activity, there was provision for the almost direct generation of evaluative data in Examples 3.5, 5.1, 5.4 and 5.6. There was facility to embed evaluative enquiry in Examples 5.7, 6.1, 6.4 and 7.2.

Generalizations

I have inferred that a suitable way of finding out about the effectiveness of teaching is to discover what the learning outcomes are. It has been implicit in at least three examples in this chapter (Examples 10.2, 10.3 and 10.6) that, with new or even subtly different learning outcomes in mind, new or different methods of assessment and of evaluation are necessary in order to identify or measure them validly. Suitable methods for assessment and evaluation must always be sought and used, if reliable outcomes are desired.

In Example 10.4 in particular, but also from other points in this text where I have written of mismatches, I have suggested that we should be wary of relying merely on the opinions of students (or of teachers) about the effectiveness of a given situation or method, in achieving the desired outcomes.

I thus offer three fairly simple thoughts at this point:

- If we pinpoint what it is that matters to us as teachers in a teaching and learning situation, it is then not too difficult to find direct ways of observing or extracting data which informs us about that outcome, or its absence.
- Structures for formative evaluation can soon usefully become part of the weft and weave of the design of the teaching and learning activity, and will then continue to inform the teacher constructively, even as the very process of learning is progressing.
- Questionnaires can be a shallow, suspect and naive way of seeking the evaluative information we require, but – when they are well designed and the evidence they yield is corroborated – they can be a source of useful data.

Comments

Many of the examples described in this chapter have concentrated formatively and usefully, I hope, on the scrutiny of events during a learning experience or a closely linked sequence of learning experiences. They have had these features:

- All of the enquiries sought to extract information which would be of use to a particular teacher, taking a particular course with particular students; no attempt was made to extract generalizable findings.
- All but one of the investigations which have been described took place where there had been a radical change in teaching methods, and where (perhaps regrettably) there was no attempt to distinguish between differences which arose

due to novelty, and differences which might be a feature of learning under the new arrangement, once it was well-established.

- All examples concentrated on the immediate learning or learning experience, or on the learners' behaviour while learning or doing.
- The enquiries entailed evaluative activity which took place as near as possible to the event, and was usually not retrospective by more than 30–45 minutes.
- In two of the examples (10.7 and 10.8), enquiry was in two steps – with the second stage of enquiry digging deeper and more meaningfully into the detail of the learners' experiences.
- There was often a careful emphasis on getting the learners to describe a particular piece of action or an outcome, and not to generalize, philosophize, describe rhetorical daydreams or give a global view of their thinking.
- There was often an attempt to triangulate the information given by the learners with their observed behaviour.

Before you test this, some second thoughts from me

1. One factor which often militates against the introduction of new teaching methods with new goals is that the educational system may still retain old methods of assessment whose hidden curriculum perpetuates the status quo. In trying to measure or identify the results of new teaching methods in pursuit of changed objectives, one of the most acute challenges we have to face is that we are obliged to devise and obtain acceptance for appropriate methods of assessment – or, worse still, may be expected by the Establishment and the status quo to use inappropriate but established methods which consequently generate meaningless or misleading data or, worse still, encourage shallow learning.
2. If we eventually succeed in devising suitable instruments of enquiry, our tests then serve both for formative enquiry and in summative assessments. In the latter, they figure as an additional encouragement to learners for development in the directions indicated to them by the hidden curriculum of our novel assessment scheme. This development will thus only be in the directions we desire – provided the methods of assessment are appropriate. How can we ensure that? *Can* we ensure that?
3. And can we ensure objectivity in our observations, and in what they record? In the circumstances described in my first quartet of examples, the learners had a subtle appreciation of what the teachers were expecting. So it is quite possible that the learners' descriptions of what they were doing were a reflection of the teachers' expectations – rather than of the reality of learning behaviour. (This is an issue which would be a highly relevant worry in Examples 10.6 and 10.7.) In addition, you may wish to consider how much we are entitled to assume, from what is possibly wishful thinking, about how learners' thinking is influenced by teaching; and how safely we can extrapolate from that, to the conclusions inferred in some of my summaries. There are sound reasons, in other words, for questioning the objectivity or even the potential for objectivity in much of the methodology I have described in my examples.

4. Several of the examples I have given also raise an interesting fundamental question with regard to the ownership or leadership in the search for the type of information a teacher requires, both to provide summative assessments and, formatively, to inform and shape the process of curriculum development. Given all that I have written earlier (Chapter 7) about the influence of self-assessment on learning, why have I not relied more on the learner, as a self-assessing and self-aware person, in the examples I have quoted and in the methodologies of evaluation I have suggested, and which you may choose to adopt? It is arguable that evaluation based solely on enquiry by teachers or researchers cannot ever be sufficiently well informed about the thoughts and feelings of learners to provide or inform authoritative conclusions. Should we not be moving even more to schemes in which it is the learner who provides us with those sound self-evaluations of the learning which is within the individual – evaluations which we, the teachers, will then only have to audit before we make use of them?

Dear John

My first attempts to harness the power of reflection seem to be going fairly well, and rather as you predicted. That's understandable, I suppose, because I've just been trying to follow your examples.

But I want to do more than that, and I would hope in so doing to avoid rediscovering the educational wheel. With respect, which as usual means precisely the reverse of that, I feel that what I've read so far is distinctly Cowan-centred. I need to profit now from what others have done and written. I need to encounter a broader perspective and range of experiences than you can provide on your own.

Where should I read about other work in this field?

11

Where Should You Read about Other Work in This Field?

Introduction

Please don't expect this chapter to be a delayed and overdue literature survey on the topic of supporting the reflective learner. It will simply offer you a list of my suggestions for some further reading which you may wish to undertake, coupled with comments about why I recommend that particular choice. I have compiled it with the intention of providing rather more in the way of other perspectives than I have offered so far through the second thoughts which I have inserted at the end of each chapter.

I have tried to identify writings, particularly in books, which I believe to have something worthwhile to offer to you. I give few references to published papers, since I know that it can be time-consuming and sometimes frustrating to chase these up. But I point you towards texts which in turn provide references to articles describing individual innovations which may be of interest and use to you. I see this chapter as beginning a reflective loop in which we should both ponder over what we have covered so far, think about the gaps and perhaps the biases in that, and hence move into a consequent surge of activity, on your part, based on some of the further reading which I describe and which I hope I may attract you to explore.

I make no apologies for concentrating on Rogers, Boud and Gibbs – since these are the trio of writers whom I see as the authorities in this field, whose work has been most useful to me and whom I expect to be equally useful to you.

Coverage

What, then, are the topics worthy of broader coverage than you have encountered so far in this somewhat anecdotal journey of ours? First and foremost, there is the whole matter of *reflection,* which is the process on which both my argument and my method have been based. Linked to reflection, there is a concept which I have hardly named, commonly described as *metacognition* – which is that thinking about thinking which detaches us from immediate action, to observe how we do things, to evaluate how well we do them, and to suggest possible ways of improving. Most of my examples of learning and facilitative teaching involve metacognition each time students go into the loops of my Cowan diagram.

I have written fairly definitely about what I have distinguished as two contrasting emphases in reflection. These are the analytic reflection which bridges from particular experiences to the generalizations which we can apply in similar situations; and the evaluative reflection which contributes greatly to metacognition. I expect that you will wish to find out what others have written and thought, and essentially what others have done as teachers in their pursuit of effective *reflection by learners*. In an extension of that enquiry, I suggest that you should similarly examine activity in the practice of *self-assessment*, which has had a great deal of attention in recent years, and has also figured in my examples.

Implicit in much of my approach to innovation over the years has been that style of enquiry by learners and teachers which I have called action-research. In simple terms, when I engage in action-research, it tells me a lot about *me* teaching *my* subject to *my* students in *our* situation; but it doesn't tell me much about teaching in general. (The proper way to describe that distinction, incidentally, is to talk about the type of study which leads to idiographic rather than nomothetic findings.) I prefer the colloquial explanation of the term, and hope that it is sufficiently clear to you. I expect that you will wish to think about the use and usefulness of the *action-research* approach in higher education.

Underlying almost everything I have described, of course, I have blandly assumed the worth of *student-centred learning*. I feel that it behoves me at this point to suggest how you can confirm the value of this approach, and of its inevitable implications in respect of a move towards *facilitation* of learning.

That set of already familiar topics provides the framework for my responses to the question which heads this chapter. I will be (openly this time) putting a bundle of questions into your mouth under most of the following headings, and then leaving it to you to find your own answers from the texts I recommend – and elsewhere. Here, then, is our agenda for this chapter:

1. student-centred learning – and facilitation
2. reflection
3. metacognition
4. learning situations which depend on reflection
5. self-assessment
6. action-research.

That is a formidable list. So let's begin without further ado, with the first item.

11.1   Student-centred learning – and facilitation

Our questions under this heading should include:

- When, why and with what promised outcomes is student-centred learning desirable and effective?
- Why and when is it to be preferred to instruction, with the teacher being in control and taking authority?
- What does it entail?
- When facilitation is assumed, what is then the role of the teacher?
- How can an old-style teacher change to an entirely different approach?

If some or all of these questions are important to you at this point, I strongly recommend the writings of Carl Rogers as the place to begin further reading. Rogers worked and theorized on the facilitation of effective and deep learning. He offers us a rationale for student-centred learning, and then leaves it to each of us to formulate our own generalizations and plan accordingly.

At a relatively early stage in his long professional career, Rogers brought together what he regarded as his most important writings, in a volume called *On Becoming a Person* (Rogers, 1961). He explained how he had built up his whole approach to his work, both as a therapist and as a teacher. He distinguished firmly between simple knowledge of facts (such as who won the battle of Bannockburn or when the umpteenth opus by Beethoven was first performed) and what he had described as significant learning. His approach had been based on the idea that learning is significant when it is functional, and pervades the person and their actions. That sounds to me the type of person-centred process which those who espouse learner-centred learning seek to facilitate through reflection.

Over the years, though, the book which has had most influence on my style and ideas as a facilitator has been *Freedom to Learn* (Rogers, 1969). In its time this was an inspiration for many like myself, who yearned to improve on the educational status quo, without being quite sure how to go about that monumental task. The full title, tellingly, was *Freedom to Learn – A View of What Education Might Become*. Rogers gave me, and many other teachers of that generation, a vision of what our students' learning might become. He used helpful examples in plenty to convey his concepts and principles; and so he armed us to experiment, without being entirely dependent on our own resources while doing so.

Sadly I cannot refer back to that early volume nowadays, because I gave away my last copy to an enthusiast – and then found that the replacement which I purchased (Rogers, 1983) was in many ways a totally different volume. It has a different title – *Freedom to Learn for the 80's* – and vastly changed content, in that more than half was completely rewritten. I commend this later volume to you, even if your library has a copy of the early version – because the differences, and in particular the additional experiences which Rogers was able to draw on, seem to me to be significant.

But I confess that there is at least one omission in the new text which I regret. Arguing in the first version for the principles on which his approach to teaching was based, Rogers listed his ten principles for good learning, followed by ten guidelines for the teacher who would facilitate that kind of active learning. Over the years, I have paraphrased Rogers' principles, putting them into the first person and asking teachers, as I now ask you, 'Which of these statements would *you* say are true, of *your* learning?' Please take a minute or two now, just to check through your answers to these questions about how *you* learn:

- Have you a natural potential for learning?
- Do you learn more significantly, when what you are learning is relevant?
- Do you find it threatening to be expected to change your view of yourself?
- When such threats are minimized, is it easier for you to learn?
- Do you find it easier to be perceptive when you are not under pressure?
- Do you learn significantly by doing?
- Do you learn better when you take responsibility for your own learning?
- Do you learn most lastingly when your feelings are involved, as well as your intellect?
- Are you more independent, creative and self-reliant when evaluation by others is secondary?
- Is 'learning to learn' the most socially useful learning for you in the modern world?

If you have answered 'Yes' more often than 'No', I suggest that you have just confirmed that you believe in learner-centred learning, for yourself at least, and hence that you should be committed to facilitative teaching. I presume you will expect many other adults to share that view – with you, and with Rogers.

In his rewritten book, Rogers (1983) could firmly claim that much research had by then provided hard evidence that his person-centred approach had led to all of his hoped-for or promised outcomes – admittedly mainly in schools, but still with lessons for those like me who see education as a continuum. He gives references in respect of these claims and their justification, and also includes many detailed reports from teachers who had put his ideas into practice.

Rogers concentrated, both in his therapy and in his teaching, on situations which he intended to be growth-promoting, and devoted to the development of the person. With that goal in mind, he was convinced that as a teacher he should:

- enter a unified or integrated relationship with each learner, as what he chose to call a *congruent* person;
- demonstrate *unconditional positive regard* for the learner, accepting each one and caring for them as separate person;
- experience an *empathic understanding* of the learner's world, as seen from the inside.

These three conditions for developing Rogers' facilitative style transfer naturally into learning and teaching situations in higher or further education. However, they are complex and abstract concepts, derived from the world of psychotherapy. Consequently they may perturb or confuse you. Perhaps it will assist if I illustrate what he meant, using examples I have already described in this book. For instance:

In the several Interpersonal Process Recall examples I have described, teachers were courageously prepared to unearth their immediate thoughts and feelings, and to make these available to their students without editing or censoring. That demonstrated their congruence with their learners. *Congruence* is perhaps best captured by the sense of what Rogers called transparency. Transparency in teaching means that teachers make themselves transparent to the learner, who can then see right through to what the teacher actually is, within their relationship. When a teacher is a real person with students in this kind of way, being what he or she is and entering into a relationship with them without presenting a front or a facade, then the teacher is acting as a congruent person and – as the teachers in my examples soon discovered – the facilitation of learning is much more likely to be effective.

You may recall the description I gave of the situation when I decided to ask my student subjects to analyse their own protocols of problem-solving, and then to report what they had learned from that about their thinking. Sometimes the students described remarkable approaches which I could easily have received with evident astonishment or (worse still) a reaction which questioned the soundness of their method. If and when I received what they told me with genuine interest and with a willingness to explore their worth, then I was displaying *unconditional positive regard*. This is expressed when the teacher has a positive and accepting attitude to whatever the student is, or is thinking or doing, at that moment. It is a prizing of learners as imperfect human beings, whether they display occasional apathy, erratic desires to explore byways of learning, or engage in sporadic efforts to achieve major goals. It generates a positive response from learners (Rogers, 1983), as I have learned when I have taken Rogers on trust, and tried to follow his principles.

In the learning journal examples I have described in this book, the teachers who provided comments in which there was no element of judgement and a clear desire to understand what the learners were reporting, implicitly established their desire to assimilate and empathize with what they were reading. *Empathic understanding* goes further than unconditional positive regard. It requires that the teacher accurately senses and assimilates the feelings and personal meanings which the student is communicating, and in turn communicates that understanding back to the student. I always found it heartening that, when my students moved on to the next year of their course in which a reflective journal was not a requirement, some few asked if they could go on keeping journals and if I would continue to provide empathic comments. Not many students volunteer to do coursework which is not a requirement. I learned first from the journal pages and then from the students' subsequent reactions, that reflection and empathic comments were judged by these students to be a positive influence on their commitment to learning, and on their lives.

Rogers contended that when teachers display their understanding of the meaning of the learning experience for their students in these three interrelated ways, learning improves (Rogers, 1980). That was a stark contrast with the behaviourist theories of learning which were being advanced and widely followed at the time he wrote. In 1962, Rogers met with Skinner for a dialogue before 500 people (Kirschenbaum and Henderson, 1990). This lengthy debate brought together the respective leaders, at that time, of the schools of humanist and behaviourist psychology. Skinner, the behaviourist, had committed himself to the purposeful reinforcement of observable behaviour as the way to bring about learning, and thus to enhance teaching effectiveness. Rogers, in contrast, had concentrated his approach to teaching and learning on the person-to-person relationship. If you are wrestling with the distinction between instruction and teacher-led education on the one hand, and facilitation and learner-centred learning on the other, I recommend that you dip into the Skinner versus Rogers debate in Kirschenbaum and Henderson (1990). You will find much on which to ponder, especially the role of freedom in learning, the difference between control and influence, and the value of genuineness. The other debates in the same text are also a useful way of testing out the Rogerian approach.

However, I would be remiss if I only offered you Rogers for your further reading. So I also recommend a thought-provoking collection of relatively early papers on the experience of learning, in a volume of that title (Marton *et al.*, 1984). This helpfully addresses the fundamental questions about what students learn, and how that learning takes place. It also establishes a sound base for studying the work which has been carried out in recent years on the important difference between deep and surface learning, two terms whose meaning is, I hope, almost self-evident. In this connection, Entwistle and Ramsden (1983) provide a subsequent account of researches into different approaches to learning, and point out the implications for those university teachers who wish to improve the effectiveness of their teaching. Ramsden (1988) offers a further volume of contributions which open by covering research taken into practice, and go on to action and reflection – all based on the view that teaching should be directed towards helping students to understand. (You will note that helping is the everyday word for facilitating.) Ramsden (1992) firmly promotes the view that effective teaching in higher education involves listening to students, and changing how we think about teaching. I suggest that you will find this particular book helpful if you want to pursue the notion of learner-centred learning.

You may also find it useful to read the contributions which Boud (1981) has assembled around the theme that the role of teachers is not simply to transmit knowledge, but also to assist their students to take increasing responsibility for their learning. That is a slightly different, but complementary, justification for learner-directed learning. In a text which confirms the relevance of this perspective, Morgan presents his reflections on experiences of study (Morgan, 1993). He takes his readers into a position where they view learning from the student perspective – which I found thought-provoking.

However, Gibbs is my preferred writer for my own current needs. He presents with characteristic directness the arguments for a new approach to improving the quality of student learning (Gibbs, 1992), and goes on to describe the work of people who have applied in their teaching these arguments, and the principles emerging from research into learning. The evaluations which he presents with these case studies are, I feel, distinctly persuasive. Gibbs has been a powerful influence on teachers in higher education over the past two decades. He offers clear justification for change to student-centred approaches, and helps teachers who are so persuaded to see how they can achieve that radical step, in their own situations. I would advise you to extend your reading of him beyond this one publication.

Finally, you may find it valuable to become acquainted with the texts of Paulo Freire (Taylor, 1993). Taylor has written a stimulating account of Freire's 'Metodo' – that method which depends on the practice of freedom in learning, facilitated by teachers who ask questions and who prompt further action in response to the learners' answers. This has messages to prompt your reflection if you aspire to facilitate worthwhile learning.

11.2   Reflection

Although the questions themselves are straightforward, I'm afraid I find it difficult to formulate advice to you about where to find adequate answers under this heading. You certainly should wish to know:

- Where can you read about theories of reflection, and their relevance to higher education?
- What do we know of how reflection operates and how it can be stimulated?
- What impact can reflection have on which aspects of the learning process?

To be frank, theories are thin on the ground, unsubstantiated by hard data, and yet are held and followed by some – perhaps including myself – with passionate conviction. So how can you pursue these issues? I suggest that it will be helpful to begin your further study of this topic from Boud and Walker (1991). These writers have assembled, as part of a course on adult learning in the workplace, a fine set of readings to provide a foundation for your subsequent thinking and development about reflection.

From that beginning, the key sources under this heading are easy to identify, of course. They include Kolb's much quoted (but less often read) seminal text (1984). This somewhat weighty treatment of the theory is helpfully summarized in everyday language, and accompanied by ideas for practice, in a handbook by Gibbs (1988). He translates the theory of experiential learning into an attractive reality for teachers and students. Gibbs answers the second and third of our questions as clearly and succinctly as any writer I have encountered.

Next comes Schön. It is important to note that Schön set out initially to address the need to educate reflective professionals in situations where theory and practice needed to be properly integrated. He saw learning and development as ensuing when reflection led the practitioner to extract understanding from the problems which had arisen or were arising in professional practice. That is not quite the type of situation with which most teachers in higher education work.

Schön's work is summarized in the two key texts which have already been mentioned (Schön, 1983, 1987). These have been usefully carried forward by Schön (1991) in a volume which provides a helpful range of illustrative case studies which depend on reflection. The central notion in this text is of a reverse educational approach suited to facilitate reflection. It begins by asking what practitioners need to know; it then presumes that the answer begins from reflection on the understanding which they have already acquired from everyday practice. Nevertheless it troubles me that the practitioners in the case studies are often seen as subjects for research, rather than as thoughtful and developing researchers of their own practice.

For an alternative and yet acceptably profound account of the development of reflective judgement, you may find it helpful to read King and Kitchener (1994). They detail the stages which lay the foundation for encouraging reflective thinking by adults, and which lead to the development of reflective judgement. Another alternative perspective comes from Handal and Lauvås (1987), who treat reflection as being at the heart of teacher education. Their writing should stimulate your thoughts, if you are prepared to consider the transfer of their philosophy to your own discipline and situation.

In recent years, the text on reflection from experiential learning which I myself have found most thought-provoking is Weil and McGill (1989). They introduce and edit contributions given originally to the First International Conference on Experiential Learning. In particular, they present a stimulating analytical argument which differentiates between four 'villages' of experiential learning, and some of the practices, challenges and influences associated with each. I will not attempt to summarize their analysis, but I encourage you to find time to read it and think through its implications for you and your work.

11.3 Metacognition

For non-specialist readers, Entwistle (1992) sets out a clear summary of the relationship between metacognition, styles of learning and theories of learning, which you should find useful as an advance organizer for your reading in this area. You can also find an alternative introduction, in everyday terms, in the Open University Resource Pack for courses E530/730 (Thompson, 1992). Pask's complex work on metacognition has been summarized by Entwistle (1978), which is perhaps a better access for the uninitiated to his thinking than Pask's own writings provide.

Metacognition, in simple terms, means thinking about thinking. My colleague, Helen Wood, shares with her students the idea of the monkey she has on her shoulder – which offers comments to her, on her thinking and doing, just as Pask's observer (Example 6.2) does; it is a feature of her own thinking about her thinking. That metaphorical monkey, like Pask's observer, is initiating metacognition. Similarly, when learners reflect (with or without prompting) on a recent experience while they are following the Kolb cycle, and when they try to identify what they were doing in that experience, they are engaging in metacognition. And when learners reflect-in-action, and notice, for example, illogicalities or errors in their thinking, then they are devoting time, however briefly, to metacognition.

Metacognition entails an awareness of your own cognitive processes, and so it should lead you to make a conscious and selective choice and use of cognitive strategies in particular situations. I take reflection, as we have encountered it to date in this book, as being a subset of metacognition. For metacognition need not necessarily arise from a recent experience, or even from one particular experience, though that is generally the case in Kolbian and Schönian reflection, as I have described them. It can be treated as a focus for teaching – and be integrated into an undergraduate teaching programme, as Woods (1994) and Biggs (1985) have done. This school of educational practice maintains that deep learning develops when adults devote time to analysing and talking about their learning and their learning strategies, and are prompted to do so in interventionist programmes which establish the existence of alternative or supplementary strategies which it might be worth considering, or testing out. My own work with students who had studied and analysed their problem-solving led them inexorably to explore the potential of strategies favoured by their classmates (Cowan, 1986a). I therefore allocated time deliberately to the facilitation of just such general metacognition, in terms which did not relate directly to one particular experience. The learning outcomes were tangible for my students.

If you are interested in taking the topic of metacognition further, and in doing so from a theoretical basis, a starting point could be Marton *et al.* (1984), although I would tend to persuade you to favour the more integrated combination of theory and practice to be found in Richardson *et al.* (1987). Alternatively, Biggs and Moore (1993) present the whole concept and possibility as a central component in effective teaching for deep learning and the development of abilities.

11.4   Learning situations which depend on reflection

The questions here should include:

- To what extent can reflection on process be encouraged?
- With what outcomes?
- How do teachers go about introducing this new practice, and optimizing the return from its use?
- Are there other approaches to developing transferable abilities?

As usual, I will try to point you towards sources which contain a range of examples, to help you to find your own answers from within them. So I advise you to read first in Gibbs (1988). This slim volume illustrates the theory with persuasive examples, and in turn justifies the examples by providing a theoretical basis for them. You will find it especially helpful that the first examples are categorized according to the phase of the Kolb cycle with which they are primarily concerned. All are transferable, and none are complex. There then follow a set of clearly explained case studies which are taken from particular disciplines and situations, but which offer many transferable suggestions. I hope you will appreciate, as I do, his frank closing discussion of the problems which a teacher can face in moving to experiential learning. I find this book refreshingly relevant to my needs.

A booklet which should be of direct assistance to you has been written, for staff development purposes, by Baume and Baume (1992). They set out to help university teachers to design programmes and courses which depend on active, and reflective, learning. The basis for that approach is detailed in lucid and practical terms. Practising lecturers from a range of disciplines then describe how they themselves have used active learning in their course. Finally (in a separate publication) they provide resources for staff development workshop activities based on these ideas.

Next on my list for you, I would suggest a return to Weil and McGill (1989) for the wealth of examples which they include, all within a helpful framework for teachers like you and me. Kolb and reflection figure heavily in this text. The writers begin by trying to make sense, as they put it, of the diversity of theory and practice to be found in the field called experiential learning. Then they group contributions which deal with the processes of coming to know yourself, inside and outside educational institutions. A range of innovative developments in post-school education follow, after which they look at the power of experiential learning literally to transform society. Finally, there is a view forward, into the future.

I would also urge that you consider spending time on Gould and Taylor (1996). They write from the innovative background of social work education, in which many creative ideas have been developed in the past two decades. They offer a varied and useful account of cases in which the concept of reflective learning has been applied to education in their discipline area. Their book presents material from both academic and practice settings, each of which features reflective learning. I benefited greatly from the reflective and theoretical discussions which are part of most of the papers, and the examples have had much to offer me; I hope they have the same impact for you.

Next I must mention two publications in the series 'New Directions for Teaching and Learning' from which I have taken much for myself. Hutchings and Wutzfdorff (1988) of Alverno College have assembled some good examples of learning through experience, together with a helpful review of assumptions and principles. This makes easy but authoritative reading. A companion volume by Stice (1987) adds further complementary examples.

Reflection is implicit in many of the case studies included by Boud (1988) in his book on developing student autonomy. For that reason it will make useful reading for you, especially from the point of view of promoting constructive second thoughts. For the discussion of the issues surrounding autonomy is relevant to reflection, as to many other aspects of teaching and learning. That discussion leads on to the presentation of a number of case studies in which reflection is not specifically addressed, but where it features strongly and in interesting ways. The same is true of the examples offered by Ramsden (1988), which you should expect to prompt you to the same analytical and reflective style of reading – again pushing you (like me) to broaden your thinking to extend to teaching in general, and not merely to supporting the reflective learner.

If you seek to read more comprehensively, and to continue to relate reflection to your teaching in general, you should read Boud and Griffin (1987). This is an interesting and original text which approaches, through the contributions of a range of writers, the question of what learning is like *for those who are learning*. It contains teachers' reflections on learning prompted by their practical experiences of learning and of teaching, which are reported almost incidentally. There are chapters here which deal with aspects of learning which are usually neglected, such as intuition and how interdependence is conceived and learned. There are also chapters which concentrate on personal learning and growth; and there are chapters which deal with the experience of those who return to study. Finally, the editors return to their two main and linked topics – learning, and the facilitation of learning. The theme of reflection runs through this book; I often take it down from my shelf, to be prompted into new lines of thought. If you find it helpful as a teacher to concentrate more on learning than on teaching, I would also encourage you to read a subsequent and highly original publication (Boud *et al.*, 1993) which emphasizes the role of personal experience in learning, through contributions in which the various contributors have tellingly written themselves into the experiences they describe and analyse.

You should find it helpful to relate learning based on facilitated reflection to other approaches in current use by exploring the literature on problem-based learning, especially when it includes examples of learning in which reflection figures. You could make a start on this topic from Boud (1985). This again contains a mixture of case studies which provoke reflection through the contrasts they provide.

I warmed to the examples given by Tresman and Edwards (1993), in this case specifically for science education. And so I offer you my last suggestion, in the hope that you will be prepared to grapple with mathematics – though not necessarily to contemplate teaching that subject. Mason has devoted much effort to the creation of situations in which learners have to move rapidly from generalizations to speculations and specialized conclusions, which are tested out in new particular situations – and hence back again into generalizations. He set this up for his Open University colleagues, as I have already mentioned, in a special course unit for the foundation course in mathematics of that time (Mason, 1984). The approach is expanded in a companion volume (Mason *et al.*, 1982), from which I have never failed to draw encouragement and inspiration. I hope it can do that for you, too.

11.5   Self-assessment

I reluctantly digress into semantics. Boud (1995), who is the leading authority in this field, often writes of self-assessment; yet most of the practice he describes, or includes in the accounts he has commissioned from other teachers, is of what I prefer to call self-evaluation. That distinction is important to me here, whatever words we use. Boud's self-assessment, which I would myself describe as evaluation, does not contribute to the overall grading or mark for the student concerned. Indeed, he declares that self-assessment 'has the self as agent and audience' and 'is essentially formative and not absolute, although it can be used for summative purposes'. I hope you will be prepared to continue, for at least the short time which remains while we are together, to accept a usage in which I employ 'evaluation' to describe a *process* in which judgements are made by comparing performance with criteria or standards; and if I restrict the term 'assessment' to evaluation which concentrates on an *outcome*, in the form of a grade or mark or judgement, whether formative or summative. Whatever the titles we use, I submit that the distinction between an emphasis on process and an emphasis on outcome is significant.

Evaluative reflection often inexorably encourages the learner to follow a process which leads to a self-assessment of learning – which is a new and for some teachers a worrying possibility. For the teacher and the examination board have long had absolute authority to judge, grade and mark learners and learning. So there are natural grounds for concern whenever anyone suggests engaging learners in self-*assessment* – and this apprehension does not disappear if the innovators strive to make it clear that they will not be abdicating from the responsibility to provide the marks or grades which will contribute ultimately to certification.

I expect you will already have discerned my personal enthusiasm for self-assessment, and thus will wish to formulate a more detached and better informed judgement than you are yet in a position to make. If so, I suggest that your questions under this heading should include:

- To what extent are self-evaluation and self-assessment currently encouraged by teachers?
- With what outcomes?
- Beyond the range of examples in this book, how can teachers go about persuading students to be frank with themselves and others about their worth, and to engage in an activity which some students will see as a responsibility for their teachers?

I have difficulty offering you sources on self-assessment other than those edited by Boud, in which you will fortunately find a great variety of views and experiences. I can only mention inadequately that Rowntree (1977), writing at the beginning of the period in which this approach began to find favour, had some far-sighted comments. And that Heywood (1989), writing on assessment ten years later, includes tellingly frequent references to self-assessment, although he does not deal with it as a separate topic.

The issues of practice and outcomes are thoroughly addressed by Boud (1995). I recommend this to you, partly for his keen interest in this aspect of higher education, and partly for the varied contributions by other teachers and researchers who have first-hand experience of self-assessment and its outcomes. The book begins with a personal statement by Boud himself, which I find frank and persuasive. It then moves into a clinical review of the state of the art, which is well illustrated by examples from the wide range of different disciplines, cultures and teaching styles in which it has figured. It concludes with another testimony by Boud, which is again written very much in the first person, and is a fine example of 'transparency'.

Boud's opening description (1995: 1) seems to me to endorse much that the rationale behind the Cowan diagram, as I have described it in these pages, seeks to attain:

> Whenever we learn, we question ourselves. 'How am I doing?', 'Is this enough?', 'Is this right?', 'How can I tell?', 'Should I go further?' In the act of questioning is the act of judging ourselves and making decisions about the next step. This is self-assessment.

Boud goes on to declare the assumptions about self-assessment on which his thinking is founded. These are that self-assessment is a necessary skill for lifelong learning, that it needs to be developed in university courses, and that it is necessary for effective learning. He then makes the significant point that the conditions which promote reflection are very much those which promote self-assessment (and vice versa?). He lists these conditions as:

- active engagement with a task which is accepted as having learning as its primary purpose;
- a task which includes significant elements of choice by the learner, which matter for learning;
- an experience which is not predictable by the learner, who is encouraged to notice surprises within it;
- a challenge of some sort to the learner's experiences;
- the learner having to make choices and follow them through;
- the new learning having to be linked, by the learner, to the old learning.

Interesting case studies in this text include self- and peer marking in a large electronics class; self-assessment against declared criteria in engineering design; self- and peer assessment of class participation in law; and an example of self-assessment in negotiated learning in science education. In addition, there is a helpful review of several self-assessment initiatives which stemmed from the UK Enterprise in Higher Education funding, and which relate to several different domains. But there is one surprising omission from the coverage – namely the extensive use of self-assessment in the established course structure at Alverno College, and the comparably extensive evaluative research which demonstrates the impact of self-assessment on the learning there (e.g. Loacker *et al.*, 1986).

I have some reservations about the chapter on research into self-assessment, which appears to me to dwell rather more than I would have expected on reliability and associated factors, given Boud's earlier statements about the self-relevance of the process. I would not quibble with his judgement that much of the research is 'both conceptually and methodologically unsound'. But if an effort is to be made to rectify that weakness, I would make a plea for it to dwell more than hitherto on the effects of self-assessment on learning outcomes and potential – ahead of reliability, whose importance I nevertheless do not dispute.

11.6   Action-research

There is, for me, no distinct line dividing the formative evaluation of teaching from action-research; there is more in the way of a grey area where one type of activity shades into the other. With that caveat, let me nevertheless try to distinguish the two concepts, and establish my use of the terms, as usual by examples.

I am engaged in formative evaluation:

- when I get my students to draw concept maps of their learning, and compare what that tells me with my objectives for the tutorial in which we have just taken part;
- when I collect feedback questionnaires which ask about the strengths and weaknesses of the comments I make on their submitted work;
- when I pre-test and post-test my students after I have presented an explanation in a new way, and wish to find out how well it has been understood.

I am engaged in action-research:

- when I get a colleague to interview my students to learn which aspects of my teaching style are helpful to them;
- when I use Interpersonal Process Recall to discover something of how my students react to my teaching;
- when I use workshop-style activities to discover the learning needs which my students perceive, so that I can respond to them in my subsequent work with that group.

I take formative evaluation to be an investigation of learning and of the learning experience, undertaken, perhaps with the help of a colleague or my students, with the express purpose of obtaining data which will tell me where there is need or scope for improvement in what I do. I take action-research to include formative evaluation, but to cover also those investigations in which I merely set out to learn more about the nature of the immediate learning and of the learning experiences for which I am responsible.

The concept of the teacher as researcher of their own practice has a well-established pedigree. Around 1970, a number of educational leaders advanced the argument for the teacher to be truly professional in responding to the need to research the outcomes of their practice. A prominent writer on this theme was Stenhouse (1975, 1984). In (school) teacher training and education, the approach has gained considerable acceptance (e.g. Heywood, 1992). But university teaching, for which until recently there has been no rigorous training or preparation, has been predictably reluctant to move onwards from intuitive development and so-called evaluation – which often amounts to little more than the administering of questionnaires designed by untrained amateurs and summarized without being analysed.

Only a few years ago there was perhaps but one text to which any university teacher interested in evaluating beyond the self-devised questionnaire approach might be referred – and that was the handbook by Cross and Angelo (1988) of what in the United States is called classroom assessment techniques. This publication followed a provocative paper by Cross (1986) in which she had quoted Schön (1983), who had asserted that the questions driving research into teaching and learning did not seem to be the questions for which answers were truly needed to improve professional practice. In attempting to connect practice and research, Cross proposed that research on teaching and learning should be carried out in literally thousands of classrooms, by the teachers themselves. *Classroom Assessment Techniques*, (Cross and Angelo, 1993), now in a second and expanded edition, has gained in its revision a much enlarged introduction to the process of classroom assessment. It now offers a definition, a rationale, a teaching goals inventory, five steps to a successful start, and advice on planning and implementation. It then lays out twelve case studies, before suggesting methods of enquiry which you, the average university teacher and reader, might use in your own classroom enquiries.

A companion volume (Cross and Steadman, 1996) is designed to be used by university teachers in groups and in workshops. In a case method approach, it illustrates how teachers can think about a variety of common learning issues, focusing on how students are learning, and on such issues as motivation, deep and surface learning, metacognition and critical thinking.

My initial advice to you is that you should begin from this Cross collection; you will find much that you can use, and much cause to widen your horizons about what we as university teachers should and can be doing in the way of action-research. If you then decide to limit your activity by concentrating simply on formative evaluation, you could focus your list of possible strategies or 'tools of enquiry' by obtaining two publications produced principally for teaching staff of the Open University (Cowan and George, 1997; Hewitt *et al.*, 1997) or the popular booklet from Gibbs *et al.* (1988).

If full action-research is a line that you wish to pursue further, then I can warmly recommend three texts which have been of great use to me. Hopkins (1993) has written a sound guide for those who wish to undertake research in their classrooms. The fact that he writes for a readership who are mainly engaged in school teaching seems to me to be unimportant. Certainly I find his advice directly relevant to me, whether I seek to enhance my teaching, to test the assumptions of educational theory, or to evaluate new developments. Winter (1989) has written a similar style of text, free from jargon and rooted in practicalities, which sets out to encourage and advise practitioners who want to understand and improve their work, and in rather more detail than Hopkins offers. I would suggest that you sample both, and choose to begin from the one which appeals most to you, on a first skim reading, and once you have defined the questions for which you seek answers.

Last, but for me the most important, there is a handbook of methods and resources for the reflective practitioner which I rate highly as a storehouse of ideas, theories and principles (McKernan, 1996). If you make any sort of commitment at all to action-research or rigorous formative evaluation, I would advise you to buy this one, keep it handy and use it often. It is strong on the philosophy, methodology and analysis of action-research.

Finally, some second thoughts from me

Try to find time to read the work of Perry (1970). He assembles from his research a nine-step scale of intellectual and ethical development, which has been much used in educational research. Perhaps the most significant outcome of his reported findings and their effect on others is that many teachers have been shocked, like Perry, to discover the intellectual immaturity of their own students, and remain puzzled about how to find ways to enable these students to make progress upwards, in the direction of qualitatively sounder conceptions of learning and of the process of learning. You can make speedy acquaintance with Perry's work in a chapter (Perry, 1988) in Ramsden's book, which I have already mentioned in another connection. You should also, however, find time for the intensely thought-provoking book by Belenky and colleagues (1986) which has its origins in the fact that almost all of Perry's reported work was with male students. These women writers describe how they set out with the same aim as Perry, but a different method and outcomes. They wanted to focus on themes which might be more prominent among women learners, and on what women learners have to say about the development of their minds. This led the writers to a classification of knowledge as received, subjective, procedural or constructed – to which I cannot do justice in a brief summary. It remains in my thinking as something which surely does not only relate to female adult students; I hope you may find it useful in prompting similar second thoughts on your part.

These two sources are where I would suggest you start, in looking once again, I hope, for the facilitation of your second thoughts. Equally fruitful will be the ample and easily accessible literature on learning styles (e.g. Schmeck, 1988), which is something this book has barely touched on, and which lies at the heart of that individuality in learning which is one of the main justifications for providing learner-centred learning which copes with individual needs and styles.

A Postscript: Final Reflections

On the structure of this text

In these pages I have told stories about the *experiences* of myself and others in educational innovations, many if not all of which contain examples and non-examples to illustrate my points. Through the comments which I have made after telling my stories, I have hoped to encourage you to engage in your own *reflection*, rather than to follow *my* process of reflection, which led me – years ago – to my own conclusions. For I have hoped with all my heart that you would reach your own conclusions and *generalizations*, from your own thinking and in your own words. You see, I was confident that, if you just went on to test out some of your generalizations (as opposed to mine), or were stimulated by mine, then the plan for the *testing* would become yours. And thus the *next experiences*, as you moved on from this text, would certainly be yours, in joint ownership with your students.

You will have noticed from what I have written (and indeed from the subtitle of this book), that I regard reflection as a key issue for teachers who want to help students to develop (relevant) competencies and abilities. I believe that it is over the bridge of Kolbian reflection that particular experiences travel, to be transformed into the generalizations which are of use well beyond the limitations of whatever is the current teaching and learning context. I believe that it is detached Schönian reflection which inspires us to move forward to new goals with a purposeful and meticulous self-management of our learning and development.

Reflection is also critical, from the point of view of the proactive teacher, because most learners don't know how to reflect. They find it difficult to understand what reflecting entails, and so they encounter considerable difficulties when we make demands on them, which call on them to reflect. It is relatively easy for a teacher to plan teaching and learning situations which begin from experiences. It is not too difficult to present a new generalization, and encourage learners to find ways to test it. That is one of the many aspects of teacher training, for example, which has been extremely well addressed by Heywood (Heywood, 1992). But, wherever learners may enter the Kolb cycle, I have never found it easy to provoke or structure their reflection when they reach that stage in the cycle, which is why that part of the teacher's task has taken up so much of my text and of our reflections.

What of your own reflection, then? I wonder if you have been prompted by the structure of my text to reflect. I wonder if the questions I have asked, and left for you to answer, have been provocatively facilitative – or merely frustratingly provocative. If it was the latter, please get in touch with me at the publisher's address, and help me to improve the text for those who may come after you.

On the questions which I chose to answer

A troublesome point in this text for me (and perhaps for you) has been the choice, and the introduction, of the questions which have headed the various chapters. Although there has been a pretence of dialogue in my presentation, it has been distinctly Socratic – in the sense that I myself have set up the questions. Thus the responses offered are, I am afraid, in the sad tradition of Socratic stooges, who seldom challenged what the great master said to them.

But I am no philosopher. So what I have written should be sharply scrutinized, and its weaknesses, assumptions and omissions should be identified and challenged. That is something which I am aware has (understandably) been done inadequately by my alter ego – he who pops up in the second thinking at the end of each chapter. He knows me too well and has lived with me so long that he thinks in my way, asks second-thought questions which matter to me, and tends to agree with my conclusions.

But *you* shouldn't do that. I hope you didn't – and won't.

On what I've missed out

Postman and Weingartner (Postman and Weingartner, 1971) argued that the ability to identify and ask good questions is the best measure of the quality of someone's education. I hope you've been identifying and asking good questions during your reading here – and especially that you have been asking yourself questions which go beyond those that I have chosen to address. Helen Wood, who has often been a source of both strength and inspiration for me in the past ten years, reflected very deeply when I asked her to come up with an example of an ability which really mattered in her discipline. She offered me that description which I have often quoted subsequently – namely the ability to notice what is not there. This is an ability which is at once important and demanding, as Sherlock Holmes explained to Dr Watson following the curious incident of the dog in the night-time. For the dog did nothing in the night-time – which was the curious incident, of course.

You will have found it relatively easy in your reflections on this text to notice, in what was there, the things that you didn't agree with, or the assumptions with whose justification you were dissatisfied. But I hope you also looked for what wasn't there. And I earnestly encourage you, in this, my last prompting of your reflection, again to give that search your earnest attention – as you emerge from the experience which I hope this text has created for you.

References

Agnew, M.S. and Cowan, J. (1986) Exchanging experiences, in *Proceedings of The Freshman Year Experience 1986*. Columbia, SC: University of South Carolina.

Angelo T.A. and Cross, K.P. (1993) *Classroom Assessment Techniques*. San Francisco: Jossey-Bass.

Anon. (1980) *Education for Capability Manifesto*. London: Royal Society of Arts.

Baume, C. and Baume, D. (1992) *Course Design for Active Learning*. Sheffield: CVCP Universities' Staff Development and Training Unit.

Belenky, M.F., Clinchy, B.M., Goldberger, N.R. and Tarule, J.M. (1986) *Women's Ways of Knowing*. New York: Basic Books.

Biggs, J.B. (1985) The role of metacognition in enhancing learning skills, *Proceedings of the Annual Conference of the Australian Association for Research in Higher Education*. Hobart: AARHE.

Biggs, J.B. and Moore, J.P. (1993) *The Process of Learning* (3rd edn). Sydney: Prentice-Hall of Australia.

Bligh, D.A. (1971) *What's the Use of Lectures?* Exeter: D.A. and B. Bligh.

Bligh, D.A., Ebrahim, G.J., Jaques, D. and Warren Piper, D. (1975) *Teaching Students*. Exeter: Exeter University Teaching Services.

Bloom, B.S., Engelhart, M.D., Furst, E.J., Hill, W.H. and Krathwohl, D.R. (1956) *Taxonomy of Educational Objectives, Handbook I: Cognitive Domain*. New York: David Mackay.

Boud, D.J. (ed.) (1981) *Developing Student Autonomy in Learning*. London: Kogan Page.

Boud, D.J. (ed.) (1985) *Problem-Based Learning in Education for the Professions*. Sydney: HERDSA.

Boud, D.J. (ed.) (1988) *Developing Student Autonomy* (2nd edn). London: Kogan Page.

Boud, D.J. (1995) *Enhancing Learning through Self Assessment*. London: Kogan Page.

Boud, D.J. and Griffin, V. (1987) *Appreciating Adults Learning: From the Learners' Perspective*. London: Kogan Page.

Boud, D.J. and Walker, D. (1991) *Experience and Learning: Reflection at Work*. Victoria: Deakin University.

Boud, D.J. and Walker, D. (1993) Barriers to reflection on experience, in D.J. Boud, R. Cohen and D. Walker (eds) *Using Experience for Learning*. Buckingham: SRHE and Open University Press.

Boud, D.J., Cohen, R. and Walker, D. (eds) (1993) *Using Experience for Learning*. Buckingham: SRHE and Open University Press.

Boyd, H.R. and Cowan, J. (1986) A case for self-assessment based on recent studies of student learning, *Assessment and Evaluation in Higher Education*, 10(3): 225–35.

Boyd, H.R., Adeyemi-Bero, A. and Blackhall, R.F. (1984) *Acquiring Professional Competence through Learner-directed Learning*, in Occasional Paper No. 7. London: Royal Society of Arts.

Brohn, D.M. (1973) A test of structural understanding, in Conference on 'Concrete Objectives for Education'. Slough: Cement and Concrete Association.

Brohn, D.M. and Cowan, J. (1977) Teaching towards an understanding of structural behaviour, *The Structural Engineer*, 55(1): 9–18.

Brown, G.A. (1996) Referee's comment on an early draft of this text.

Cowan, J. (1974a) The essential features for a successful academic game, *SAGSET Journal*, 4(2): 17–22.

Cowan, J. (1974b) Identification of standard game forms with definable objectives, *Programmed Learning and Educational Technology*, 11(4): 192–6.

Cowan, J. (1975) 'The feasibility of resource-based learning in civil engineering', PhD thesis, Heriot-Watt University, Edinburgh.

Cowan, J. (1977) Individual approaches to problem-solving, *Aspects of Educational Technology*, Vol. X. London: Kogan Page.

Cowan, J. (1980a) Improving the recorded protocol, *Programmed Learning and Educational Technology*, 17(3): 160–3.

Cowan, J. (1980b) Freedom in the selection of course content – a case study of a course without a syllabus, *Studies in Higher Education*, 3(2): 139–48.

Cowan, J. (1980c) Quantitative and qualitative understanding of engineering phenomena, *Proceedings of Ingenieur Padagogic '80*, 113–19.

Cowan, J. (1981a) Design education based on an expressed statement of the design process, *Proceedings of the Institution of Civil Engineers*, Part 1, 70: 743–53.

Cowan, J. (1981b) The Truss game, *Simulation/Games for Learning*, 11(2): 92–5.

Cowan, J. (1982) Ascending order questions, *Civil Engineering Education (ASEE)*, 4(2): 7–10.

Cowan, J. (1983) How engineers understand, *Engineering Education*, 13(4): 301–4.

Cowan, J. (1984a) Beyond instruction, *Proceedings of the 6th International Conference on Higher Education*. Lancaster: University of Lancaster.

Cowan, J. (1984b) *Acquiring Professional Competence through Learner-Directed Learning*, in Occasional Paper No. 7. London: Royal Society of Arts.

Cowan, J. (1984c) Learning from mistakes – a pragmatic approach to Education for Capability, *Programmed Learning and Educational Technology*, 21(4): 256–61.

Cowan, J. (1986a) Education for Capability in engineering education, DEng thesis, Heriot-Watt University.

Cowan, J. (1986b) Are we neglecting real analytical skills in engineering education? *European Journal of Engineering Education*, 11(1): 67–74.

Cowan, J. (1988) Struggling with self-assessment, in D.J. Boud (ed.) *Student Autonomy in Learning*. London: Kogan Page.

Cowan, J. (1989) Four fatal errors equals two lessons learnt, *Education and Training Technology International*, 26(2): 145–8.

Cowan, J. (1994) Sauce for the goose? A multi-level pedagogical pilot, *Education and Training Technology International*, 31(4): 325–9.

Cowan, J. (1995) Research into student learning – Yes, but by whom?, in S. Törnkvist (ed.) *Teaching Science for Technology at Tertiary Level*. Stockholm: Royal Swedish Academy of Engineering Sciences.

Cowan, J. and George, J.W. (1989) Non-numerate study skills: a mathematical approach, *Open Learning*, 4(1): 41–3.

Cowan, J. and George, J.W. (1992a) How was it for you? *The New Academic*, 1(2): Spring, 20–1.

Cowan, J. and George, J.W. (1992b) Diminishing lists of questions – a technique for curriculum design and formative evaluation, *Education and Training Technology International*, 29(2): 118–23.

Cowan, J. and George, J.W. (1993) A toolkit of techniques for formative evaluation by tutors, Paper to ICDE Conference on Quality Assurance in Open and Distance Education. Cambridge: ICDE.

Cowan, J. and George, J.W. (1997) *Formative Evaluation – Bordering on Action Research*. Project Report 97/5 Edinburgh: The Open University in Scotland.

Cowan, J. and Harding, A.G. (1986) A logical model for curriculum development, *British Journal of Educational Technology*, 2(17): 103–9.

Cowan, J. and Morton, J. (1993) MOCO – A structural game for undergraduates, *Programmed Learning and Educational Technology*, 10(4): 267–73.

Cowan, J., Morton, J. and Bolton, A. (1973) An experimental learning unit for structural engineering studies, *The Structural Engineer*, 51(9): 337–9.

Cross, K.P. (1986) A proposal to improve teaching, *AAHE Bulletin*, September: 9–14.

Cross, K.P. and Angelo, T.A. (1988) *Classroom Assessment Techniques*. Michigan: National Center for Research to Improve Postsecondary Teaching and Learning.

Cross, K.P. and Angelo, T.A. (1993) *Classroom Assessment Techniques* (2nd edn). San Francisco: Jossey-Bass.

Cross, K.P. and Steadman, M.H. (1996) *Classroom Research: Implementing the Scholarship of Teaching*. San Francisco: Jossey-Bass.

Davies, I.K. (1971) *The Management of Learning*. London: McGraw-Hill.

Entwistle, N.J. (1972) Students and their academic performance in different types of institutions, in H.J. Butcher and E. Rudd (eds) *Contemporary Problems in Higher Education*. London: McGraw-Hill.

Entwistle, N.J. (1978) Knowledge structures and styles of learning; a summary of Pask's recent research, *British Journal of Educational Technology*, 48: 1–11.

Entwistle, N.J. (1992) *The Impact of Teaching on Learning Outcomes in Higher Education*. Sheffield: CVCP Universities' Staff Development and Training Unit.

Entwistle N.J. and Ramsden, P. (1983) *Understanding Student Learning*. London: Croom Helm.

Fordyce, D.S.E. and Cowan, J. (1985) Developing the fundamental cognitive abilities appropriate to engineering education, *Proceedings of SEFI 1985 Conference*. Madrid: SEFI.

Garry, A.M. and Cowan, J. (1987) To each according to his needs, *Aspects of Educational Technology, Vol. XX*. London: Kogan Page.

Geddes, C. and Wood, H.M. (1995) *The Evaluation of Teaching Transferable Skills in Science*. Project Report 95/1. Edinburgh: The Open University in Scotland.

George, J.W. (1992) Alverno College; a learner's perspective, *British Journal of Educational Technology*, 22(3): 194–8.

Gibbs, G. (1987) Private conversation on methods of bringing about innovation.

Gibbs, G. (1988) *Learning by Doing*. Sheffield: Further Education Unit.

Gibbs, G. (1992) *Improving the Quality of Student Learning*. Bristol: Technical and Education Services.

Gibbs, G., Habeshaw, S. and Habeshaw, T. (1988) *53 Interesting Ways to Appraise Your Teaching*. Bristol: Technical and Educational Services.

Gould, N. and Taylor, I. (1996) *Reflective Learning for Social Work*. Aldershot: Arena.

Handal, G. and Lauvås, P. (1987) *Promoting Reflective Teaching*. Milton Keynes: SRHE and Open University Press.

Hewitt, P., Lentell, H., Phillips, M. and Stevens, V. (1997) *Open Teaching Toolkit: How Do I Know I Am Doing a Good Job?* Milton Keynes: The Open University.

Heywood, J. (1989) *Assessment in Higher Education* (2nd edn). Chichester: Wiley.

Heywood, J. (1992) Student teachers as researchers of instruction, in J.H.C. Vonk and H.J. van Hielden (eds) *New Prospects for Teacher Education in Europe*. Association for Teacher Education in Europe. Brussels: Vrije Universiteit, Amsterdam.

Hirschhorn, L. (1991) in D.A. Schön (ed.) *The Reflective Turn*. New York: Teachers College, Columbia University.

Hopkins, D. (1993) *A Teacher's Guide to Classroom Research* (2nd edn). Buckingham: Open University Press.

Hutchings, P. and Wutzdorff, A. (eds) (1988) *Knowing and Doing: Learning Through Experience*. San Francisco: Jossey-Bass.

Kagan, N., Krathwohl, D. and Miller, R. (1963) Stimulated recall in therapy using videotape: a case study, *Journal of Counseling Psychology*, 24: 150–2.

Keller, F.S. (1968) Goodbye teacher . . ., *Journal of Applied Behavioural Analysis*, 1: 79–89.

King, P.M. and Kitchener, K.S. (1994) *Developing Reflective Judgment*. San Francisco: Jossey-Bass.

Kirschenbaum, H. and Henderson, V.L. (eds) (1990) *Carl Rogers Dialogues*. London: Constable.

Kolb, D.A. (1984) *Experiential Learning*. Engelwood Cliffs, NJ: Prentice-Hall.

Leith, G.O.M. (1969) *Second Thoughts on Programmed Learning*. London: National Council for Educational Technology.

Lewin, K. (1951) *Field Theory in Social Sciences*. New York: Harper and Row.

Loacker, G., Cromwell, L. and O'Brien, K. (1986) Assessment in higher education; to serve the learner, in C. Adelman (ed.) *Assessment in Higher Education*. Washington, DC: US Office of Education.

McAleese, W.R. (1996) Telephone conversation with the writer, gratefully acknowledged.

McKernan, J. (1996) *Curriculum Action Research* (2nd edn). London: Kogan Page.

Marton, F., Hounsell, D. and Entwistle, N.J. (eds) (1984) *The Experience of Learning*. Edinburgh: Scottish Academic Press.

Mason, J.H. (1984) *Learning and Doing Mathematics*. Milton Keynes: The Open University.

Mason, J.H., with Burton, L. and Stacey, K. (1982) *Thinking Mathematically*. Wokingham: Addison-Wesley.

Mentkowski, M. and Strait, M.J. (1983) *A Longitudinal Study of Student Change in Cognitive Development, Learning Styles and Generic Abilities in an Outcome-centered Liberal Arts Curriculum*. (NIE-G-77–0058). Milwaukee: Alverno Productions.

Milne, A.A. (1926) *Winnie-the-Pooh*. London: Methuen.

Morgan, A. (1993) *Improving your Students' Learning*. London: Kogan Page.

Parlett, M. and Hamilton, D. (1972) *Evaluation as Illumination: A New Approach to the Study of Innovatory Programmes*. Edinburgh: Centre for Research in Educational Sciences, University of Edinburgh.

Pask, G.B. (1975) *The Cybernetics of Human Learning and Performance*. London: Hutchinson.

Perry, W.G. (1970) *Forms of Intellectual and Ethical Development in the College Years*. New York: Holt, Rinehart and Winston.

Perry, W.G. (1988) Different worlds in the same classroom, in P. Ramsden (ed.) *Improving Learning – New Perspectives*. London: Kogan Page.

Postle, D. (1993) Putting the heart back into learning, in D.J. Boud, R. Cohen and D. Walker (eds) *Using Experience for Learning*. Buckingham: SRHE and Open University Press.

Postlethwait, S.N., Novak, J. and Murray, H.T. (1964) *An Integrated Experience Approach to Learning*. Minneapolis: Burgess.

Postman, N. and Weingartner, C. (1971) *Teaching as a Subversive Activity*. Harmondsworth: Penguin.

Ramsay, A.B. (1956) Epitaph on a syndic, in J.M. Cohen (ed.) *More Comic and Curious Verse*. Harmondsworth: Penguin.

Ramsden, P. (ed.) (1988) *Improving Learning – New Perspectives*. London: Kogan Page.

Ramsden, P. (1992) *Learning to Teach in Higher Education*. London: Routledge.

Rainier, T. (1980) *The New Diary*. London: Angus and Robertson.

Richardson, J.T.E., Eysenck, M.W. and Warren Piper, D. (1987) *Student Learning*. Milton Keynes: SRHE and Open University Press.

Rogers, C.R. (1951) *Client-centred Therapy*. Boston, MA: Houghton Mifflin.

Rogers, C.R. (1961) *On Becoming a Person*. Boston, MA: Houghton Mifflin.

Rogers, C.R. (1969) *Freedom to Learn*. Columbus, OH: Merrill.

Rogers, C.R. (1983) *Freedom to Learn for the 80's*. Columbus, OH: Merrill.

Rosier, N. (1998) *Faxes up North*. Project report (un-numbered). Edinburgh: Open University in Scotland.

Rowntree, D. (1977) *Assessing Students: How Shall We Know Them?* London: Harper and Row.

Schmeck, R.R. (ed.) (1988) *Learning Strategies and Learning Styles*. New York: Plenum Press.

Schön, D.A. (1983) *The Reflective Practitioner*. New York: Basic Books.

Schön, D.A. (1987) *Educating the Reflective Practitioner*. San Francisco: Jossey-Bass.

Schön, D.A. (ed.) (1991) *The Reflective Turn*. New York: Teachers College, Columbia University.

Skemp, R.R. (1971) *The Psychology of Learning Mathematics*. Harmondsworth: Penguin.

Skemp, R.R. (1979) *Intelligence, Learning and Action*. Chichester: Wiley.

Stenhouse, L. (1975) *An Introduction to Curriculum Research and Development*. London: Heinemann.

Stenhouse, L. (1984) Artistry and teaching: the teacher as focus of research and development, in D. Hopkins and M. Wideen (eds) *Alternative Perspectives on School Improvement*. Lewes: Falmer Press.

Stice, J.E. (1987) *Developing Critical Thinking and Problem-Solving Abilities*. San Francisco: Jossey-Bass.

Taylor, P.V. (1993) *The Texts of Paulo Freire*. Buckingham: Open University Press.

Thompson, J. (1992) E530/730: Resource Pack Section 2 – *Your Learning Journey*. Milton Keynes: Open University.

Tresman, S. and Edwards, D. (1993) Reflecting on practice: some illustrations, in E. Whitelegg, J. Thomas and D. Tresman (eds) *Challenges and Opportunities for Science Education*. Milton Keynes: The Open University.

Vygotsky, L.S. (1978) *Mind in Society*. Cambridge, MA: Harvard University Press.

Weedon, E.M. (1994) *An Investigation of the Effect of Feedback to Students on TMAs*. Project report 94/5. Edinburgh: Open University in Scotland.

Weil, S.W. and McGill, I. (1989) *Making Sense of Experiential Learning*. Buckingham: SRHE and Open University Press.

Winter, R. (1989) *Learning from Experience*. Lewes: Falmer Press.

Woods, D.R. (1987) in J.E. Stice *Developing Critical Thinking and Problem-Solving Abilities*. San Francisco: Jossey-Bass.

Woods, D.R. (1994) *Problem-based Learning: How to Gain the Most from PBL*. Hamilton, Ontario: McMaster University Bookstore.

Index

The Society for Research into Higher Education

The Society for Research into Higher Education (SRHE) exists to stimulate and co-ordinate research into all aspects of higher education. It aims to improve the quality of higher education through the encouragement of debate and publication on issues of policy, on the organization and management of higher education institutions, and on the curriculum, teaching and learning methods.

The Society is entirely independent and receives no subsidies, although individual events often receive sponsorship from business or industry. The Society is financed through corporate and individual subscriptions and has members from many parts of the world.

Under the imprint *SRHE & Open University Press*, the Society is a specialist publisher of research, having over 80 titles in print. In addition to *SRHE News*, the Society's newsletter, the Society publishes three journals: *Studies in Higher Education* (three issues a year), *Higher Education Quarterly* and *Research into Higher Education Abstracts* (three issues a year).

The Society runs frequent conferences, consultations, seminars and other events. The annual conference in December is organized at and with a higher education institution. There are a growing number of networks which focus on particular areas of interest, including:

Access	Learning Environment
Assessment	Legal Education
Consultants	Managing Innovation
Curriculum Development	New Technology for Learning
Eastern European	Postgraduate Issues
Educational Development Research	Quantitative Studies
FE/HE	Student Development
Funding	Vocational Qualifications
Graduate Employment	

Benefits to Members

Individual

• The opportunity to participate in the Society's networks

- Reduced rates for the annual conferences
- Free copies of *Research into Higher Education Abstracts*
- Reduced rates for *Studies in Higher Education*
- Reduced rates for *Higher Education Quarterly*
- Free copy of *Register of Members' Research Interests* – includes valuable reference material on research being pursued by the Society's members
- Free copy of occasional in-house publications, e.g. *The Thirtieth Anniversary Seminars Presented by the Vice-Presidents*
- Free copies of *SRHE News* which informs members of the Society's activities and provides a calendar of events, with additional material provided in regular mailings
- A 35 per cent discount on all SRHE/Open University Press books
- Access to HESA statistics for student members
- The opportunity for you to apply for the annual research grants
- Inclusion of your research in the *Register of Members' Research Interests*

Corporate

- Reduced rates for the annual conferences
- The opportunity for members of the Institution to attend SRHE's network events at reduced rates
- Free copies of *Research into Higher Education Abstracts*
- Free copies of *Studies in Higher Education*
- Free copies of *Register of Members' Research Interests* – includes valuable reference material on research being pursued by the Society's members
- Free copy of occasional in-house publications
- Free copies of *SRHE News*
- A 35 per cent discount on all SRHE/Open University Press books
- Access to HESA statistics for research for students of the Institution
- The opportunity for members of the Institution to submit applications for the Society's research grants
- The opportunity to work with the Society and co-host conferences
- The opportunity to include in the *Register of Members' Research Interests* your Institution's research into aspects of higher education

Membership details: SRHE, 3 Devonshire Street, London
W1N 2BA, UK. Tel: 020 7637 2766. Fax: 020 7637 2781.
email: srhe@mailbox.ulcc.ac.uk
world wide web: http://www.srhe.ac.uk./srhe/
Catalogue: SRHE & Open University Press, Celtic Court,
22 Ballmoor, Buckingham MK18 1XW. Tel: 01280 823388.
Fax: 01280 823233. email: enquiries@openup.co.uk

USING EXPERIENCE FOR LEARNING

David Boud, Ruth Cohen and David Walker (eds)

This book is about the struggle to make sense of learning from experience. What are the key ideas that underpin learning from experience? How do we learn from experience? How does context and purpose influence learning? How does experience impact on individual and group learning? How can we help others to learn from their experience?

Using Experience for Learning reflects current interest in the importance of experience in informal and formal learning, whether it be applied for course credit, new forms of learning in the workplace, or acknowledging autonomous learning outside educational institutions. It also emphasizes the role of personal experience in learning: ideas are not separate from experience; relationships and personal interests impact on learning; and emotions have a vital part to play in intellectual learning. All the contributors write themselves into their chapters, giving an autobiographical account of how their experiences have influenced their learning and what has led them to their current views and practice.

Using Experience for Learning brings together a wide range of perspectives and conceptual frameworks with contributors from four continents, and is a valuable addition to the field of experiential learning.

Contents

Contributors
Lee Andresen, David Boud, Angela Brew, Stephen Brookfield, Ruth Cohen, Costas Criticos, Kathleen Dechant, Elizabeth Kasl, Victoria Marsick, John Mason, Nod Miller, John Mulligan, Denis Postle, Mary Thorpe, Robin Usher, David Walker.

208pp   0 335 19095 2 (Paperback)